16 Writing Lessons to Prepare Students for the State Assessment and More

Engaging Lessons with Planning Sheets and
Evaluation Checklists to Help Students Master the Essentials
of a Short, Focused Writing Assignment

by
Mary Lynn Woods

SCHOLASTIC
PROFESSIONAL BOOKS

NEW YORK • TORONTO • LONDON • AUCKLAND • SYDNEY
MEXICO CITY • NEW DELHI • HONG KONG • BUENOS AIRES

DEDICATION
For Ken with love forever

ACKNOWLEDGMENTS

Sometimes words don't adequately convey the depth of gratitude felt by an author toward the many individuals who helped pilot a curricular dream, clarify thoughts during the writing process, organize and edit text for publication, and last but not least, provide encouragement during discouraging moments and confidence during doubt-filled times. For this support, I wish to thank the following people:

Jenny Stapp, Fishback Creek Public Academy, Metropolitan School District of Pike Township, Indianapolis, Indiana; Kelly Wilson, Central Elementary School, Lebanon Community Schools, Lebanon, Indiana; Molly Seward, Snacks Crossing Elementary School, Metropolitan School District of Pike Township, Indianapolis, Indiana; Betsy Dulhanty, Perry-Worth Elementary School, Lebanon Community Schools, Lebanon, Indiana; Adam Spencer, Central Elementary School, Lebanon Community Schools, Lebanon, Indiana; Andy Seward, Zionsville Lower Middle School, Zionsville Community School Corporation, Zionsville, Indiana; Mary Kay Hunt, Cynthia Kattau, and the fifth and sixth grade teachers of Metropolitan School District of Warren Township, Indianapolis, Indiana; and Wendy Murray and Merryl Maleska Wilbur of Scholastic Inc.

Cover design by Maria Lilja
Cover photo by Vicki Kasala
Interior design by Solutions by Design, Inc.
Interior photo courtesy of the author.

Excerpt from ONE-MINUTE BEDTIME STORIES by Shari Lewis with Lan O'Kun.
Copyright © 1982 by Shari Lewis.

ISBN 0-439-36548-1

Table of Contents

Introduction

This book provides sixteen easy-to-follow, reproducible writing lessons that you, the classroom teacher, can use as your language arts lessons for three or more weeks. The lessons are centered on a writing assignment that requires students to know both how to apply state writing rubric criteria and how to apply knowledge of the writing process. As a result, these lessons have the potential to improve achievement on the writing portion of the state assessment. Even beyond the provision of specific lessons and test preparation aid, the intent of this book is to serve as a window of insight, enabling you to offer your students day-to-day, high-quality writing instruction.

In 1996, the first year that Indiana added a writing portion to its existing statewide assessment, I served as a scorer. I thought that the process of reading hundreds of papers would help me understand how our students were achieving and that the content of the papers would serve as a telltale view, revealing how teachers were teaching writing. As I began scoring, I asked: *How does this paper score in relationship to the requirements of the state writing rubric and in comparison to the anchor papers? How much knowledge of the writing process (specifically, planning, drafting, revising, and editing) is revealed in the finished composition?* Paper after paper, stack after stack, more questions emerged: *What does the student know about writing a well-crafted text? Does the student have a plan to manage this assignment?*

After scoring 1000 papers, I found that the majority received barely acceptable scores. Very few writers demonstrated adequate knowledge of planning, drafting, revising, and editing. Few knew how to write a well-crafted text that was logically structured. From this sample, I concluded that those who achieved top scores (fewer than 2 percent) must have been naturally talented writers who had become successful on their own.

I also concluded from what I had read that the papers revealed a lack of instructional support. It seemed clear to me that students weren't being taught how to write a well-developed text nor how to think critically and reflectively. There seemed to be little evidence of instruction of the writing process or of how to apply the state rubrics and standards to one's writing.

As an on-site language arts consultant, a good part of my job involves working with teachers as they seek to improve writing instruction. After reading those 1000 papers for nine grueling days, I resolved to construct a series of writing lessons that would be aimed at helping a larger group of teachers do just that—improve the quality of their writing instruction within the daily classroom curriculum.

This book provides you with a focused set of writing lessons to use with your students. The lessons are organized to span three weeks, but there are a number of ways they can be expanded, extended, and modified to provide you with long-range support for writing instruction. The lessons are built around a writing assignment model called a *snapshot*. The snapshot assignment was selected as the model because it is short and requires the writer to learn the criteria for a well-crafted text according to the state's rubric descriptors. The snapshot also requires the writer to practice using all phases of the writing process and to engage in reflection as a means of becoming a more independent writer.

The content and the delivery of the lessons is consistent, whether at fourth grade or eighth grade. Regardless of grade, every student's achievement on writing assignments should be expected to mature, moving from simple to more complex language structure, from little evidence of style to a lot of style, and from a lesser degree to a total degree of control over planning, drafting, revising, and editing. I believe that the only way to foster successful writers at all grade levels is to engage them in rich, long-term writing experiences that make continuous use of process and rubric knowledge.

Section 1 of this book serves as an overview, defining a snapshot, explaining its connection to the state rubric, and outlining an instructional plan that extends for more than three weeks.

Section 2 contains a series of sixteen, easy-to-follow lessons that can be used as a language arts plan over a span of three weeks or more. The lessons include clear-cut directions, examples for teaching demonstrations, skills-based strategies, and reproducible study sheets ready for student use. This series of lessons enables you to teach your students how to:

☀ create a well-crafted short writing assignment called a snapshot

☀ plan a snapshot by *talking it through* with a peer (a writing coach)

☀ become an effective writing coach who knows how to facilitate a peer's planning and ultimately use the coaching skills to self-coach

☀ use a short writing assignment as a means of practicing and gaining control over each phase of the writing process—selecting a topic, planning, drafting, revising, and editing

☀ reflect and talk about what is being learned—that is, use debriefing as a means of becoming a more independent writer

Section 3 provides background information for you about each phase of the writing process. This section includes detailed descriptions and instructional tips.

Section 4 explains how snapshot knowledge can be applied to the writing of a longer text. This section also includes a teacher's description of how she learned to teach short and longer writing assignments using the lessons from this book. Finally, this section includes a plan that can be used to teach students how to manage effectively the requirements of the statewide writing assignment.

Appendices include snapshot extension lessons that have been adapted for the content areas and were created by imaginative and innovative teachers with whom I have worked.

Finally, ***References*** contain two kinds of bibliographies: further readings for you, the teacher, as you consider shifting toward a writing workshop style for your classroom; and recommendations for a supplemental, classroom reference collection that can be used by students as they learn how to revise and edit.

SECTION 1

The Snapshot Assignment and the State Writing Assessment Connection

A PHOTOGRAPHER USES A GRAPHIC IMAGE TO PRESERVE A MOMENT IN TIME—capturing who was there, where and when an event took place, and what happened. Like a photo, a written snapshot depicts a small scenario in time, but it uses words rather than a graphic image to create a vivid picture in the reader's mind and to describe the who, where, when, and what of the scene.

Statewide writing assessments can be rigorous. They typically require students to know how to write a well-crafted text that meets specific mandated criteria (the descriptors of the state writing rubric) and how to apply the phases of the writing process—planning, drafting, first and second revision, and editing—to the writing task. In some states, students must demonstrate these competencies within a one-hour assessment. For several reasons, the snapshot assignment is an ideal way to help students learn to manage this challenge and to help them develop confidence about their writing in general. It provides a meaningful connection to the state assessment in the following ways:

1. The criteria used to write and evaluate a snapshot are selected from the content portion of the state rubric.

2. The brevity of the snapshot assignment is a real asset; the multiple phases and tasks of the writing process (planning, drafting, revising, and editing) are taught and learned in easily manageable segments. This brevity also means that students can receive evaluation on an ongoing and immediate basis *as* they learn. Also, a snapshot can be published quickly, providing students with feedback and a sense of completion.

3. The snapshot assignment creates a solid foundation of knowledge that can be applied to the writing of the longer text demanded by the state assessment. With snapshot craftsmanship and writing process know-how, students have the resources for writing a text with a more detailed beginning, middle, and end, and have had practice accomplishing this in brief, specified amounts of time.

One Snapshot Assignment Example and the State Writing Assessment

A S AN EXAMPLE OF HOW A SNAPSHOT CAN CONNECT TO THE STATE ASSESSMENT, take a look at the well-crafted snapshot below, written by Jacob, a fifth-grader. Then study the table on page 9. The table provides an analysis of the snapshot, which reflects the descriptors from the content portion of the state writing rubric in Indiana, where Jacob goes to school.

One Fifth-Grader's Snapshot

> My mom dragged me out of bed early this chilly, shivery morning to get ready for my paper route. As I was eating breakfast I caught a glance of my hamster's cage. Scampers is blond with brown blotches and was busy stuffing his face with seeds and grub. He picked up some wood chippings and quickly ran over to the corner of his cage and threw them in. Before he settled down he went over to the water bottle and moved it into his cozy nest in the corner. While he was moving it, he showed off his piggy self by standing on his hind legs and showing his puffy cheeks which were stuffed full of seeds and grub. When he had the water bottle right up to his cozy nest he settled down for a dreamy sleep! "And I have to go outside into the shivery, cold air! Lucky guy!" I thought to myself.
>
> Jacob, grade 5

An Analysis of Jacob's Text Based on His State's Writing Rubric

INDIANA WRITING RUBRIC	JACOB'S TEXT
☀ logical order	moves from self getting up and going to breakfast, to hamster's activities, back to self
☀ in-depth information and exceptional supporting details that are fully developed	clear description of hamster's cage and hamster's activity
☀ vocabulary choices make an explanation detailed and precise, a description that is rich, and/or an action that is clear and vivid	☀ dragged me out of bed ☀ cozy nest ☀ caught a glance ☀ showed off his piggy self ☀ busy stuffing his face ☀ settled down for a dreamy sleep ☀ before he settled down ☀ into the shivery, cold air ☀ puffy cheeks which were stuffed full of seeds and grub
☀ vocabulary choices that demonstrate control of challenging vocabulary	demonstrates control of challenging vocabulary in the use of lively verbs and high imagery phrasing Jacob coined some interesting phrases such as, *wood chippings* and *caught a glance*.
☀ fluent and easy-to-read text using varied sentence patterns and complex sentences	The text is fluent because it reads as if the author were "storytelling." Many sentences are structured differently: ☀ *My mom dragged...* and *As I was eating breakfast...* ☀ *He picked up some wood chippings...* ☀ *Before he settled down...* The variety of sentence structure holds the reader's interest. *As I was eating breakfast...*, and *While he was moving it, he showed...* indicates that the writer knows how to use sentence structure to show the passage of time.
☀ use of techniques, such as imagery and dialogue and/or humor and suspense, to convey meaning	The descriptions contain high imagery; Jacob uses a contrast between his cold, paper delivery morning and the hamster's cozy nest.
☀ a unique perspective; original, authoritative, lively, and/or exciting language (voice)	The storytelling quality of Jacob's text seems to shake hands with the reader. Thinking about the contrast between the hamster's cozy bed and the chilly, paper route morning makes the reader shiver and laugh at the same time.

Now, using your own state rubric, fill in the table below to analyze Jacob's text.

Your State Writing Rubric	Jacob's Text

An Instructional Plan

JACOB'S SNAPSHOT ABOUT HIS HAMSTER WASN'T THE FIRST ONE HE HAD written. As part of a writing workshop that his teacher, Ms. Wilson, taught during language arts, Jacob had been writing snapshots for more than three weeks. The hamster snapshot was his third.

During the first two weeks that Ms. Wilson's students wrote their first and second snapshots, she taught them strategies for writing a well-crafted text. Students worked in pairs, alternating roles as writer and writing coach. While the writer focused on how to construct a well-crafted text, the writing coach learned to listen, to facilitate a writer's thinking, and in turn to become a better informed writer. As students wrote their snapshots, they learned how to apply phases of the writing process—planning, drafting, first and second revision, and editing.

By the middle of the third week, each student was ready to write a third snapshot and prepare it for formal publication. Each student completed the process by typing the final copy of this third snapshot in the computer lab. The class then discussed and selected a title and a dedication for the collection of their snapshots. Two students volunteered to illustrate a cover, while two others collated the collection and another three students created a table of contents on the classroom computer.

When the collection was complete, Ms. Wilson inserted a letter in the front of the book, explaining to parents, grandparents, and other readers how the students developed the assignment and why the writing process is a key part of the curriculum. She also placed a feedback sheet at the end, requesting that readers write positive comments to the writers. When all this material was assembled, Ms. Wilson ran off four additional copies and stapled each booklet together. Five copies were published, one for the school library and four copies for the classroom library.

The classroom writers celebrated their first publication by reading aloud their snapshots to an appreciative audience of fellow students. Before leaving school that day, four students checked out the classroom copies to bring home.

The following tables illustrate Ms. Wilson's plans for her writing workshop. The first table, on page 12, provides an overview of the entire workshop. The second table (pages 13–16) has four parts, one for each of the workshop weeks. The plans are presented in outline form to give you an overall picture, at a glance, of how Ms. Wilson managed the workshop. Her format is geared toward teaching the workshop in a 40- to 50-minute language arts time block. However, based upon your teaching circumstances, you may choose to combine, extend, or condense these plans.

There are 16 lesson plans provided in Section 2 of this book. These lesson plans feature easy-to-follow directions and reproducible study sheets for student use, which can also be adapted for overhead transparencies. Once you have familiarized yourself with these detailed plans, you will be better prepared to use the following tables as a resource to help you adapt your own schedule.

As you modify the plans and adapt them to your own needs, it will be helpful to keep these questions in mind:

☀ What academic requirements from the state rubric and the state language arts standards need to be addressed?

☀ About how long will it take me to teach these requirements effectively?

☀ Over the three weeks plus, what specifically can I get done in a 40-minute language arts period?

☀ How will I organize the mini-lessons so that I can accomplish as much as possible?

Overview of an Instructional Plan for the Snapshot Assignment

Week #1	Introducing the Snapshot
	Lesson 1: Snapshot Components
	Lesson 2: A Writer Creates a Snapshot With Words
	Getting Started
	Lesson 3: Assessing a Writer's Feelings
	Lesson 4: Selecting a Topic and Planning
	Lesson 5: Writing the First Snapshot
	Learning to Polish
	Lesson 6: A Writer Uses Interesting, Exceptional Language
	Lesson 7: A Writer Includes a Dynamic Beginning
	Lesson 8: A Writer Includes a Tie-Up Ending
Week #2	Lesson 9: Debriefing to Become Better and Better
	Lesson 10: Fine Tuning Coaching Skills
	Lesson 11: Writing the Second Snapshot
	Lesson 12: Editing for Capitalization and Spelling
Week #3	Becoming More Independent
	Lesson 13: Second Revision and the Confidence Factor
	Lesson 14: Writing the Third Snapshot
	Lesson 15: Editing for Capitalization and Punctuation
	Lesson 16: Formal Publication and Evaluation
Week #4	Becoming More Independent (continued Monday and Tuesday only)
	Lesson 16 (continued): Formal Publication and Evaluation

WHAT REQUIREMENTS ARE ACCOMPLISHED?			
State Rubric	**Writing Process**	**Reflective Thinking Skills**	**Standards**
Ideas and Content • stays completely focused on topic and task • includes thorough and complete ideas and information ***Organization*** • organizes ideas logically ***Style*** • exhibits exceptional word usage • demonstrates exceptional writing technique ***Voice*** • effectively adjusts language and tone to task and reader	***Phases in Application*** • Selecting a Topic • Planning • Drafting • First • Revision • Informal Publication	• Each student will use reflection as a means of analyzing what he or she has experienced and learned to devise a plan for improvement. • The lesson segment is called "Debrief."	• Select a focus, an organizational structure, and a point of view based upon purpose, audience, length, and format requirements for a piece of writing. • Students write clear, coherent, and focused text. • Students progress through the stages of the writing process including planning, drafting, revising, and editing of multiple drafts. • Students use varied word choice to make writing interesting and precise.

MONDAY	TUESDAY	WEDNESDAY	THURSDAY	FRIDAY
* Teacher's Notes: *Introduce + explain:* *• Snapshot definition* *• Students will write 3 snapshots over the next 3–4 weeks of L.A. lessons.* *• Give each student a "snapshot writer" folder; each student is to put name on folder; Important: Each student is accountable for keeping all papers in folder.* *• Each writer will prepare and publish the third snapshot in a classroom book.* *• This book will be put into the school and class library and go home for parents, grandparents, and others to read and write feedback to the authors.* ***Lesson 1: Snapshot Components*** (page 21) ***Lesson 2: A Writer Creates a Snapshot With Words*** (page 24) *• Place all papers in the snapshot writer folder.* *• Debrief*	***Lesson 3: Assessing a Writer's Feelings*** (page 27) ***Lesson 4: Selecting a Topic and Planning*** (page 31) *• Place all papers in the snapshot writer folder.* *• Debrief*	***Lesson 5: Writing the First Snapshot*** (page 34) *• Review snapshot components.* *• Write snapshot including:* *• Selecting a Topic* *• Planning* *• Drafting* *• First Revision* *• Informal Publication (3 writers)* *• Place all papers in the snapshot writer folder.* *• Debrief*	***Lesson 5 continued...*** *• Informal Publication (8 writers)* ***Lesson 6: A Writer Uses Interesting, Exceptional Language*** (page 38) *• Place all papers in the snapshot writing folder.* *• Debrief*	*• Informal Publication (6 writers)* ***Lesson 7: A Writer Includes a Dynamic Beginning*** (page 42) ***Lesson 8: A Writer Includes a Tie-Up Ending*** (page 45) *• Place all papers in the snapshot writing folder.* *• Debrief*

* Italicized material represents teacher's notes to himself or herself.

WHAT REQUIREMENTS ARE ACCOMPLISHED?			
State Rubric	**Writing Process**	**Reflective Thinking Skills**	**Standards**
• Include all from Week 1. ***Language In Use*** • words have few or no capitalization errors • words have few or no spelling errors	***Phases in Application:*** • Selecting a Topic • Planning • Drafting • First Revision • Informal Publication • Editing	• Each student will use reflection as a means of analyzing what he or she has experienced and learned to devise a plan for improvement. • The lesson segment is called "Debrief."	• Include all from Week 1. • Students write using Standard English conventions appropriate to the grade level. • Students use speaking techniques, tone, volume, and timing of speech, enunciation, and eye contact for effective presentation. (Informal Publication requirements)

MONDAY	TUESDAY	WEDNESDAY	THURSDAY	FRIDAY
Lesson 9: Debriefing to Become Better and Better (page 48) ***Lesson 10: Fine Tuning Coaching Skills*** (page 51) • *Place all papers in the snapshot writer folder.** • *Debrief*	***Lesson 11: Writing the Second Snapshot*** (page 55) • *Selecting a Topic* • *Planning* • *Drafting* • *Informal Publication (3 writers)* • *Place all papers in the snapshot writer folder.* • *Debrief*	***Lesson 11: Writing the Second Snapshot continued...*** • *Informal Publication (8 writers)* ***Lesson 12: Editing for Capitalization and Spelling*** (page 59) • *Present Capitalization Strategies #1, "Proper and Common Nouns as Counterparts," and #2, "Your Very Own Personal Pronoun, I" and then edit for capitals.* • *Place all papers in the snapshot writer folder.* • *Debrief*	***Lesson 12: Editing for Capitalization and Spelling*** • *Present one or both "Think-It-Through" spelling strategies and edit for spelling.* • *Place all papers in the snapshot writing folder.* • *Debrief*	***Lesson 12: Editing for Capitalization and Spelling continued...*** • *Continue practicing the capitalization strategies and the spelling strategies.* • *Place all papers in the snapshot writing folder.* • *Debrief*

* Italicized material represents teacher's notes to himself or herself.

WHAT REQUIREMENTS ARE ACCOMPLISHED?			
State Rubric	**Writing Process**	**Reflective Thinking Skills**	**Standards**
• Include all from Weeks 1 and 2. **Style** • exceptional writing technique • writing is fluent and easy to read • writer uses varied sentence patterns and complex sentences **Language in Use** • sentences have few or no punctuation errors, few or no run-on sentences or sentence fragments	**Phases in Application:** • Selecting a Topic • Planning • Drafting • First Revision • Informal Publication • Editing • Second Revision	• Each student will use reflection as a means of analyzing what he or she has experienced and learned to devise a plan for improvement. • The lesson segment is called "Debrief."	• Include all from Weeks 1 and 2. • Use a computer to compose documents by using word-processing skills and principles of design, including margins, tabs, spacing, and page orientation.

MONDAY	TUESDAY	WEDNESDAY	THURSDAY	FRIDAY

Lesson 13: Second Revision and the Confidence Factor (page 66)	*Lesson 14: Writing the Third Snapshot* (page 72)
	 • *What Do I Already Know?*
	 • *Phases of the Process:*
	 • *Planning*
	 • *Drafting*
	 • *First Revision*
	 • *Informal Publication (3 writers)*
		Lesson 14: Writing the Third Snapshot continued...
		 • *Phases of the Process*
		  continued...
		 • *Informal Publication (6 writers)*
		 • *Second Revision*
		 • *Informal Publication (3 writers)*
			• *Informal Publication (6 writers)*
			
			 Lesson 15: Editing for Capitalization and Punctuation (page 78)
			 • *Present Capitalization Strategy # 3 and Punctuation Strategies #1–4.*
			 • *Writers edit third snapshot applying the various strategies.*
				Lesson 16: Formal Publication and Evaluation (page 84)
				 • *Students type final copy in computer lab.*
				 • *Teacher acts as Outside Editor, watching over shoulders, and monitors conducting individual conferences for:*
				  – capitalization
				  – punctuation
				  – spelling.

• *Place all papers in the snapshot writer folder.** • *Debrief*	• *Editing (capital letters)* • *Place all papers in the snapshot writer folder.* • *Debrief*	• *Editing* • *Teacher explains evaluation system and how conferencing will take place in the future.* • *Place all papers in the snapshot writer folder.* • *Debrief*	• *Informal Publication (4 writers)* • *Place all papers in the snapshot writer folder.* • *Debrief*	• *Place all papers in the snapshot writer folder.* • *Debrief*

* Italicized material represents teacher's notes to himself or herself.

WHAT REQUIREMENTS ARE ACCOMPLISHED?			
State Rubric	**Writing Process**	**Reflective Thinking Skills**	**Standards**
• Include all from Weeks 1, 2, and 3.	***Phases in Application:*** • Selecting a Topic • Planning • Drafting • First Revision • Informal Publication • Editing • Second Revision • Formal Publication	• Each student will use reflection as a means of analyzing what he or she has experienced and learned to devise a plan for improvement. • The lesson segment is called "Debrief."	• Include all from Weeks 1, 2, and 3.

MONDAY	TUESDAY
Lesson 16: Formal Publication and Evaluation continued... *(Preparation of the master copy)* • *Students vote to choose name for the collection and on the dedication.* **Small Group Work** • *Students collate the master copy (2 students).* • *Students use classroom computer to prepare table of contents (3 students).* • *Students use classroom computer to prepare cover (2 students).* • *Student uses classroom computer to prepare dedication page (1 student).* • *After school, make 4 photocopies, insert parent letter (p. 86), and bind book.*	***Lesson 16: Formal Publication and Evaluation continued...*** **Final Debrief** • *Using Lesson 3, students revise this sheet to indicate their current feelings toward writing assignments.* • *Students indicate knowledge of the writing process.* **Celebration of Authorship** • *Students read aloud final, published snapshots.* • *Enter 1 copy into school library and 4 copies into classroom library.* • *Students check out book from classroom library (4 students).*

* Italicized material represents teacher's notes to himself or herself.

16 Lessons to Teach Students How to Write Successful Snapshots

The Snapshot Assignment Incorporates the Phases of the Writing Process

T HE STATEWIDE WRITING ASSESSMENT CALLS FOR STUDENTS TO KNOW HOW to write a well-crafted text and how to apply each phase of the writing process. In some instances, students must demonstrate this knowledge within an hour. To be successful, students need to know what is involved in the structuring and crafting of text and how to manage each phase of the writing process. To help students prepare for this challenge, the snapshot assignment is set up to require the same background knowledge and application of skills.

Take a look at the table on the next page, which outlines, phase-by-phase, the tasks embedded in the snapshot assignment. As you read the table, try to imagine how a student writer might feel as he or she is taking in the breadth and scope of the tasks described.

WRITING PROCESS PHASES	TASKS THE WRITER THINKS ABOUT AND ATTENDS TO
Selecting a Topic	I am going to think of a topic (the main character and what's going on—a small scenario in time) and how much time the scenario represents.
Planning	I am going to *think about and talk through* all snapshot components with a Writing Coach (or I'll self-coach). I'll consider: ☀ Who, Where, When, and What's going on ☀ interesting, exceptional language ☀ a dynamic beginning and a tie-up ending
Drafting	I am ready to write! I am going to put my ideas down on paper. I am going to: ☀ think and write from my heart and let the words flow ☀ focus upon ideas first and editing (spelling, punctuation, etc.) later ☀ mull over in my mind interesting, exceptional language choices ☀ write a dynamic beginning and a tie-up ending ☀ attract and hold my reader ☀ feel secure enough to take risks ☀ debrief and learn from the writing experience
First Revision	I am going to make sure my snapshot makes sense and that I didn't omit any words.
Informal Publication	I am going to read my snapshot aloud to a listener. Will the listener think my snapshot makes sense? Will it hold my listener's interest?
Second Revision	I am going to reread my snapshot to find out if I need to make changes that will refine the quality of the content. I'm going to make sure that my snapshot includes: ☀ all components—Who (physical characteristics, personality, feelings), ☀ Where, When, and What's going on ☀ a fully focused topic (a small scenario in time) ☀ a logical order ☀ interesting, exceptional language that is not overdone ☀ a dynamic beginning and a tie-up ending ☀ varied sentence structure, complex and interesting sentences
Editing	I am going to reread my snapshot to correct for: ☀ capitalization at the beginning of sentences ☀ the capitalization of proper nouns (also my personal pronoun) ☀ end of sentence and middle of sentence punctuation ☀ subject/verb agreement within my sentences and paragraphs ☀ run-on sentences or sentence fragments ☀ misspelled words
Formal Publication	I am going to put my snapshot into a book for others to read. I want my readers to think my snapshot is well-crafted and that I am a competent writer. I want them to enjoy my writing.

In my experience, a typical student reaction is something like "Can I really *do all this*?" And "That's overwhelming!" is a common response even from teachers. When faced with the totality of all these tasks at one time, who wouldn't feel overwhelmed?

All kinds of classroom writing assignments overwhelm students for the same reason—in one fell swoop, they demand that a multitude of tasks be handled: "Decide what you are going to write and make a draft. Don't forget to use correct capital letters, commas, and end-of-sentence punctuation. Avoid run-on sentences. Make sure your sentence structure is varied, and by the way, be sure your spelling is correct." The net effect of this kind of instructional command is that the writer feels like things are beyond his or her control.

The problem, as I see it, can be addressed by giving the student writer a systematic way of dealing with the phases of the writing process. The lessons in this book recommend that you teach a writing assignment by showing students how to apply the writing process one phase at a time, one task at a time.

"One Phase at a Time" Lets Students Gain Control

Webster defines the word *phase* as "a successive aspect of stages in any course of change or development." I like the term, "phases of the writing process," because it conveys the notion that while engaged in a successive series of phases, the writer's thinking—and hence the quality of his or her text—changes, grows, and develops. The experience of thinking through each phase teaches the writer to understand the function of the phase and how to apply it to a text. Thus, the purpose for breaking the writing process into a series of smaller, manageable phases is to help the writer gain control.

A snapshot writing assignment provides the ideal conditions for teaching students how to apply a series of phases because it is a short assignment and easy to manage. Within three weeks, writers learn the nature of the individual phases and the skill-based tasks required by each phase. (See the table at left.)

Most of the sixteen lessons in this section include either study sheets or instructional strategies you can use to teach necessary skills. The main purpose of the instructional strategies is to provide the thinking experiences a writer needs to grasp the logic behind the skill. For this reason, I think of them as "strategies," not "activities." For example, the editing strategy in Lesson 12 teaches a writer how to edit the text for the capitalization of proper nouns. It requires the writer to analyze the distinction between the function of common nouns and the function of proper nouns. When the function of the two types of nouns is understood, the writer can more easily make correct and independent decisions now and in the future. The short text of the snapshot assignment enables learners to handle a variety of strategies because the overall assignment is so manageable.

Process, Polish, and Pride

Perhaps as teachers we undervalue the teaching of a process and over-emphasize the teaching of content. But the kind of teaching that consists primarily of the imparting of information, along with follow-up questions that require students to figure out a single correct answer, is unfortunate. This content-only instructional pattern sets students up with a 100 percent chance of being right, or a 100 percent chance of being wrong. The sting of making a mistake is highly possible. Under these conditions many students reason, "Why should I take the risk?"

Engagement in a process, however, offers students a chance to avoid the sting associated with high risk. Process writing provides students with a progression of phases in which ongoing revision serves to fine-tune the quality of the text. Phase-by-phase, the process is filled with opportunities to make changes—changes that are celebrated rather than seen as errors. Revision begins to be perceived as a welcome relief; it brings spit and polish to the text, and feelings of confidence, control, trust, and pride to the writer. Revision becomes a risk worth taking.

LESSON 1

Snapshot Components

PREPARING FOR THE LESSON

☀ Obtain a manila folder for each student to use as a writer's folder throughout the entire workshop.

☀ Select a snapshot to use as an example to show to your students. You might decide to use the snapshot on the Lesson 1 Study Sheet (page 23), or you might want to choose a photo of your own. If you do select one of your own, make sure that the content of the photo reflects information about who, where, when, and what's going on.

☀ Because it's important that each student look closely at the snapshot, you'll need to make enough copies of the photo for each student or for several small groups of students. Alternately, you might make an overhead transparency of the original photo so that all students can see it at one time.

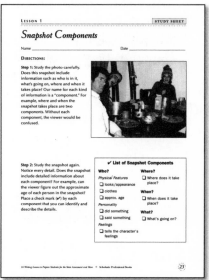

☀ Make a copy of the study sheet for Lesson 1 (page 23) for each student and a transparency of the sheet for your own use.

PRESENTING THE LESSON

1 Give each student a writer's folder and explain that all papers related to the workshop should be kept in this folder. Make clear to students that it's very important that no papers are discarded throughout the workshop. Have students write their names on their folder.

2 Keep the folders together in a secure place. Some teachers use a file box to hold folders in the classroom during the entire workshop.

3 Tell students that they are going to learn how to write a snapshot. A written snapshot is a short text using specific details so that the reader gets a vivid, clear picture in his mind.

4 Let students know that before they *write* a snapshot, they are going use a photo to learn what elements make up a good snapshot. Hold up an original photo and ask something like, "What do you expect to see in a photo?" Students might respond that they expect to see who is in it, where it takes place, when it takes place, and what's going on.

5 Hand out the Lesson 1 Study Sheet and read the Step 1 directions at the top of the sheet: *Study the photo carefully. Does this snapshot include information such as who is in it, what's going on, where and when it takes place? Our name for each kind of information in a snapshot is a "component." For example, where and when the snapshot takes place are two components. Without each component, the viewer would be confused.* Give students time to study the photo with a focus on its components.

6 Explain that part of the snapshot assignment is the "skill of observation"—students will need to be very observant and notice details. Present the second set of directions (Step 2) on the study sheet: *Study the snapshot again. Notice every detail. Does the snapshot include detailed information about each component? For example, can the viewer figure out the approximate age of each person in the snapshot? Place a check mark (✔) next to each component that you can identify and describe the details.*

Questions such as those below will help you guide a class discussion. You might use the questions as you work through Step 2 together with your students, or you could have students complete Step 2 independently and then follow up with a discussion. Some possible student responses are given in parentheses.

- ☀ Who is in the snapshot? (a grown man, a teenage boy, a girl) Discuss all physical features, such as looks/appearance, clothes, approximate age(s). Describe each in detail. (*The boy looks about 16, the girl about 12. They have on sweaters and hats so it must be cold inside. The dad or uncle has on a shirt. He looks like he's watching TV or something else.*)

- ☀ An observer deducts personality traits by studying what a character does or says. Can you determine any personality traits from this photo? (*Yes, the teenage boy is goofy and silly, a clown-type of kid.*)

- ☀ Can you determine feelings? (*The man seems distracted. The girl looks happy, and the boy is silly.*)

- ☀ What's going on? (*The family is on a ski trip; they are eating a meal.*)

- ☀ Where are they? (*They're in a hotel room, condominium, or ski lodge.*)

- ☀ What do you think it looks like outside? (*There are probably mountains and snow.*)

- ☀ When is this scene taking place? (*In winter, on a very cold day because the kids have hats on even inside.*)

Snapshot Components

Name _____   Date _____

DIRECTIONS:

Step 1: Study the photo carefully. Does this snapshot include information such as who is in it, what's going on, where and when it takes place? Our name for each kind of information is a "component." For example, where and when the snapshot takes place are two components. Without each component, the viewer would be confused.

Step 2: Study the snapshot again. Notice every detail. Does the snapshot include detailed information about each component? For example, can the viewer figure out the approximate age of each person in the snapshot? Place a check mark (✔) by each component that you can identify and describe the details.

✔ List of Snapshot Components

Who?

Physical Features

❑ looks/appearance

❑ clothes

❑ approx. age

Personality

❑ did something

❑ said something

Feelings

❑ tells the character's feelings

Where?

❑ Where does it take place?

When?

❑ When does it take place?

What?

❑ What's going on?

A Writer Creates a Snapshot With Words

PREPARING FOR THE LESSON

☀ Make a copy of the Lesson 2 Study Sheet on page 26 for each student and prepare a transparency for your use.

PRESENTING THE LESSON

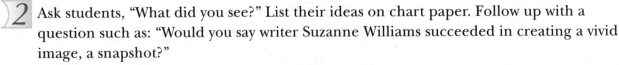

1. Explain that professional writers know how to use words to create powerful visual scenes. Instead of photographs or illustrations, a writer uses words to create a vivid snapshot in the reader's mind. Before reading aloud the following passage, ask students to listen carefully.

> *Not long after the storm, a motorcycle gang rode into town. The leader of the gang was "Bust-'em-up Bill."*
> *He was a towering six-foot-seven, and when he took off his jacket to play pool, he revealed a skull-and-crossbones tattoo that would scare the wool off the sheep.*
>
> (From *Library Lil* by Suzanne Williams, 1997)

2. Ask students, "What did you see?" List their ideas on chart paper. Follow up with a question such as: "Would you say writer Suzanne Williams succeeded in creating a vivid image, a snapshot?"

3. Hand out the Lesson 2 Study Sheet, "Snapshot Components Checklist" (page 26). Read the directions aloud: *Listen as I read aloud Williams' snapshot again. Can you name each component? Can you identify the component's details? Listen carefully as I read and place a check (✔) next to each component and detail you hear.*

4. Follow up with a class discussion based on the study sheet. Your questions and possible student responses might go something like this:

   ☀ "Who is in this snapshot?" Encourage students to point out the specific words and details Williams used to convey the appearance, personality, and feelings of the character. (*his leather jacket, the tattoo, his name—the author didn't choose "Johnny Milk Toast"*)

   ☀ "Where does this snapshot take place? Why did the writer use the phrases *scare the wool off the sheep* and *rode into town*?" (*She was making clear that this is a small farming town.*)

☀ "When does it take place? In days of old? In present times? On a sunny, warm day? In the cold of winter?" (*present times, after the storm, probably summer or spring*)

☀ "What's going on?" (*"Bust-'em-up Bill" is going into the pool hall.*) As part of this component, ask students to think about how much time transpired during this snapshot. "Is the author describing something that took place over a day? An hour? A few minutes?" It's important to help students realize that an author can write descriptively and vividly about a very short segment of time.

5 Explain that if a writer's snapshot has all the components and details for each component, the reader or listener can actually draw a sketch from the author's words. Reread Williams' snapshot and ask the students to make a sketch that includes each component and the details. The sketch can be drawn in the space allotted on the study sheet or on a separate piece of paper. Circulate around the room, encouraging students to include details in their sketches.

Here is a sample of a sketch.

6 Finally, debrief with your students. Ask questions that sum up the lesson: "What have you learned about a snapshot? Can you name the components? What's the importance of the component details?" (*The details create a mental image for the reader or listener. Without component details, reading and listening would be boring.*) Ask your students to share their answers with a partner and then with the whole class.

Snapshot Components Checklist

Name _____   Date _____

DIRECTIONS: Listen as I read aloud Williams' snapshot again. Can you name each component? Can you identify the component's details? Listen carefully as I read and place a check (✔) next to each component and detail you hear.

SNAPSHOT COMPONENTS

1 ❑ Who is in this snapshot? _____

    Physical Features   **Personality**   **Feelings**

    ❑ looks/appearance?   ❑ did something?   ❑ tells character's feelings?

    ❑ clothes?   ❑ said something?

    ❑ approximate age?

2 ❑ Where does this snapshot take place?

_____

3 ❑ When does this snapshot take place?

_____

4 ❑ What's going on? How much time does this snapshot represent?

_____

MAKE A SKETCH

DIRECTIONS: Make a sketch of the author's snapshot. Try to include all of the components and author's details in your sketch.

DEBRIEF: Ask yourself:

☀ What have I learned about a snapshot?

_____

☀ What are the components?

_____

☀ Why are the component details important?

_____

LESSON 3

Assessing a Writer's Feelings

PREPARING FOR THE LESSON

☀ Photocopy the Lesson 3 Study Sheet on page 30 for each student.

☀ Prepare a transparency of the study sheet for your own use.

☀ Make a transparency of the diagram in Section 3, "Phases of the Writing Process" (page 91).

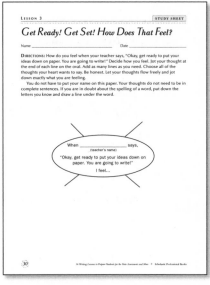

PRESENTING THE LESSON

1 Let the students know that each of them is going to write his or her first snapshot. Ask them how it feels when you say, "Okay, get ready to put your ideas down on paper. You are going to write." Explain that you want them to be completely candid and honest, that this question is not a test, not a competition, and that no one will be judged on his or her response. Some students will feel just fine. Undoubtedly others will experience nervous, uncomfortable feelings. The most common complaint from students is that they don't know how to get started. When students ask, "How many sentences are we supposed to write?" it's usually an indicator of uncertainty and nervousness about writing.

2 Share with students that even for adults, being asked to write something can often be a threatening experience. When a writer knows someone will read his or her writing, worries begin. "Will the reader think my idea makes sense? Will the reader think my spelling is wrong? Will the reader criticize me? Will the reader think I'm stupid?" Questions like these are natural, particularly among students who feel that writing is beyond their control.

3 Explain that writers seldom get the opportunity to express the true feelings that arise when they approach a writing assignment, but that in this lesson, students are going to have that chance. Distribute copies of the Lesson 3 Study Sheet and describe how to use it—as a device for expressing real feelings. Underscore that you want students to be detailed and completely honest. If it will make them feel more comfortable, they don't

have to put a name on the sheet. Emphasize that they should not worry about spelling.

It will be helpful if you model your own process of examining your feelings and of completing this activity. Using the study sheet transparency, show students how you take a moment to think about your own feelings, and then how you draw a line extending from the oval, writing your feeling or thought at the end of the line. You might also model how you would handle doubt about the correct spelling of a word—for instance, pausing, thinking, ultimately putting down those letters that you are sure of (beginning, middle, end) and underlining the word (*nervus* for *nervous* might be a good example).

Remind students that as they fill out their sheets, the class will be engaging in Sustained Silent Writing (SSW). This means the room needs to remain quiet, so quiet that the only sound should be that of pencils on paper. Allow 1 minute for them to think about their feelings and 2–3 minutes to write. Clean the transparency so that it can be used again in the next step.

4 When students have finished writing, use the study sheet transparency to share one sixth-grade class' responses. Draw lines from the oval and fill in the following eight responses. At this point, some students may wish to share their own feelings, which may be similar or identical to some of the responses on the graphic. Bearing in mind the overall comfort level of your own students, you may or may not want to elicit further responses and encourage this discussion.

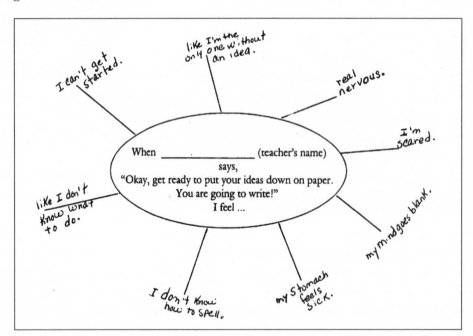

Continue by explaining that most writers have these same feelings. The feelings usually stem from a writer's sense of being overwhelmed—when facing a writing assignment, there are simply so many things to think about and do. "How can I think of my ideas, write them down on paper, spell perfectly, punctuate perfectly, get my subjects and verbs to agree perfectly, and so on—all at once?" The tasks are so demanding when layered on top of each other like this that the writer begins to feel out of control.

Reassure students that the truth is that a writer doesn't do all tasks at once, especially in the beginning. Eventually a writer may attend to multi-tasks, but in the beginning he or she concentrates on *one thing at a time*.

5   Use your overhead transparency of the writing process to discuss the phases briefly. It's best not to lecture about each phase, rather to provide a quick overview, spending no more than two minutes describing the entire chart. Remember that experience is the best teacher, and in the forthcoming lessons, your students will experience each phase of the writing process.

6   After you have presented the phases, explain that during this week and the following several weeks each student will be writing at least three snapshots. Offer students the following encouragement. You might write it on the chalkboard in a ceremonious manner and introduce it by saying, "There is something I know and feel right now that perhaps not all of you know or feel."

> Every single person in this class can write a well-crafted snapshot!
>
> I am going to teach you how to gain control over each phase of the writing process so that you can achieve writing success.

7   Finally, reveal that everybody's third snapshot will be formally published in a class booklet that will go home for parents, grandparents, and siblings to read. Highlight the "Formal Publication" phase on the transparency so that students can see how this is the culmination phase.

Remind students to place this study sheet into their writer's folders.

Get Ready! Get Set! How Does That Feel?

Name _____ Date _____

DIRECTIONS: How do you feel when your teacher says, "Okay, get ready to put your ideas down on paper. You are going to write!" Decide how you feel. Jot your thought at the end of each line on the oval. Add as many lines as you need. Choose all of the thoughts your heart wants to say. Be honest. Let your thoughts flow freely and jot down exactly what you are feeling.

   You do not have to put your name on this paper. Your thoughts do not need to be in complete sentences. If you are in doubt about the spelling of a word, put down the letters you know and draw a line under the word.

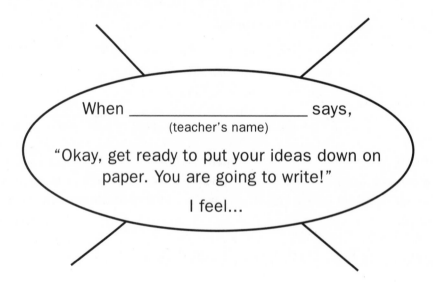

When _____ says,
(teacher's name)

"Okay, get ready to put your ideas down on paper. You are going to write!"

I feel...

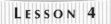

LESSON 4

Selecting a Topic and Planning

PREPARING FOR THE LESSON

☀ Make a copy of the Lesson 5 Study Sheet on page 37 for each student.

☀ Make a transparency of the study sheet for your own use.

☀ Have your transparency of "Phases of the Writing Process" available. The original is on page 91.

☀ Before the lesson, read the Section 3 subsections, "Selecting a Topic," "Planning," "Drafting," "First Revision," and "Informal Publication," on pages 90 to 101.

☀ Before you get started, read the "Teacher's Snapshot Script" on page 33. You might choose to use this snapshot script or to make up one of your own.

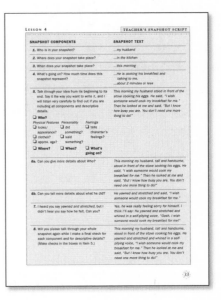

PRESENTING THE LESSON

1. Highlight "Selecting a Topic" and "Planning" on your transparency of the writing process. Inform students that most professional writers use some kind of technique to select and narrow down their thoughts on a topic and to plan the draft. Some authors mull over an idea in their heads, churning thoughts for weeks, months, and sometimes years. Others talk through the plan out loud or draw pictures before writing. Some may even use movement such as dance as a way of planning. A planning technique helps get ideas flowing and allows the writing to be more fluent, more natural.

2. Explain that, for the purposes of this snapshot writing assignment, you are going to ask students to use the technique of *talking through* to help them focus their topics and plan their drafts. This talking will occur before the writer actually writes down the idea on paper. The opportunity to *talk a snapshot through* primes the pump; it offers a writer a chance to get the ideas flowing like water out of a tap.

3. Let your students know that you are going to teach them how to work with a partner to talk through a plan. During the planning phase, one partner is called the *writer* and the other is called the *writing coach*. The writer plans by thinking about and talking through his or her snapshot. The writing coach asks questions that encourage the writer to talk about the snapshot and listens very carefully to the writer's plan. Emphasize that, during the next weeks, the goal is for each student to become an excellent snapshot writer and also a highly-skilled snapshot writing coach.

To begin, tell your students they are going to have the opportunity to act as <u>your</u> writing coach. In this lesson, you will be a writer who is narrowing down and planning a snapshot, and students will be the writing coaches who will *talk you through* your snapshot plan.

4 Give each student a copy of the Lesson 5 Study Sheet, "Writing Coach's Prompt," and place your transparency of this study sheet on the overhead. Open the lesson by explaining to them: "You are going to ask me Questions 1 through 8, but to be a skilled coach, you must know by heart the components of a well-crafted snapshot. Before you can coach me, you'll need to read items 1 through 5 carefully to review the snapshot components." Then, ask students to cover the sheet and name the components.

5 Inform students that the general topic of this snapshot is "I Saw Someone (or an Animal) Today and This Is What Happened To Him/Her." Call on individual students to ask you the questions. The task will be more manageable if you clump the questions into groups. You might say something like, "To help me narrow and focus my topic, start by asking only Questions 1 through 4." At this point, your responses should be short and without details because you are mimicking the process of a writer just beginning to grapple with an idea. You might use the "talk through" provided in the "Teacher's Snapshot Script" at right, or you might make up one of your own.

Next, have students ask Question 5 and remind them to listen carefully for all components and details. And make the following suggestion: "If I don't give enough details, use Questions 6 and 7 to get me to think and talk. Remember, the more the writer thinks and talks, the more fluent the snapshot will be."

Finally, have them ask you Question 8. Throughout this entire modeling session, demonstrate for students that you are *trying* to figure out how to say what is on your mind. For instance, you might pause often to show visible signs of thinking, saying aloud something like, "Mmmmmm, let me think. I'm not sure exactly how I want to say this." It is important to convey the notion that during planning a writer is not exactly sure of how to express an idea, but will figure it out during drafting and revising.

6 Next, ask students to focus on the item called "Debrief," which follows Question 8. Explain that a writing coach debriefs so that he or she can reflect upon what just happened and figure out how to become a better coach. Reinforce the purpose of this exercise by asking: "What are you learning from the experience of being a writing coach?" (Students might offer: "I have to be a good listener" or "I have to know the components.")

7 Conclude the lesson by asking students to predict how they think a writer will feel about beginning a draft after having had the chance to *talk a snapshot through* with a writing coach. Will they feel more confident, and if so, why?

SNAPSHOT COMPONENTS	SNAPSHOT TEXT
1. Who is in your snapshot?	*...my husband*
2. Where does your snapshot take place?	*...in the kitchen*
3. When does your snapshot take place?	*...this morning*
4. What's going on? How much time does this snapshot represent?	*...He is cooking his breakfast and talking to me.* *...about 2 minutes or less*
5. *Talk through* your idea from its beginning to its end. Say it the way you want to write it, and I will listen very carefully to find out if you are including all components and descriptive details. ❑ **Who?** *Physical Features* *Personality* *Feelings* ❑ looks/ appearance? ❑ did something? ❑ tells character's feelings? ❑ clothes? ❑ said something? ❑ approx. age? ❑ **Where?** ❑ **When?** ❑ **What's going on?**	*This morning my husband stood in front of the stove cooking his eggs. He said, "I wish someone would cook my breakfast for me." Then he looked at me and said, "But I know how busy you are. You don't need one more thing to do!"*
6a. Can you give more details about *Who?*	*This morning my husband, tall and handsome, stood in front of the stove cooking his eggs. He said, "I wish someone would cook my breakfast for me." Then he looked at me and said, "But I know how busy you are. You don't need one more thing to do!"*
6b. Can you tell more details about what he did?	*He yawned and stretched and said, "I wish someone would cook my breakfast for me."*
7. I heard you say *yawned and stretched*, but I didn't hear you say how he felt. Can you?	*Yes, he was really feeling sorry for himself. I think I'll say: He yawned and stretched and whined in a self-pitying voice, "Gosh, I wish someone would cook my breakfast for me!"*
8. Will you please talk through your whole snapshot again while I make a final check for each component and for descriptive details? (Make checks in the boxes in Item 5.)	*This morning my husband, tall and handsome, stood in front of the stove cooking his eggs. He yawned and stretched and whined in a self-pitying voice, "I wish someone would cook my breakfast for me." Then he looked at me and said, "But I know how busy you are. You don't need one more thing to do!"*

Writing the First Snapshot

PREPARING FOR THE LESSON

☀ Each student should already have a copy of the Lesson 5 Study Sheet on page 37 in his or her writing folder. In addition, you will need to have your transparency of this study sheet available.

☀ Also have available your transparency of the diagram, "Phases of the Writing Process." The original is on page 91.

☀ Before the lesson, review the Section 3 subsections, "Selecting a Topic," "Planning," "Drafting," "First Revision," and "Informal Publication," on pages 90 to 101.

PRESENTING THE LESSON

Selecting a Topic

1 Reveal to students that the moment has finally arrived—now it's *their* turn to plan and write their first snapshot. Highlight "Selecting a Topic" on your transparency of "Phases of the Writing Process."

2 Let students know that they will be using the same general topic that you modeled in the previous lesson—"I Saw Someone (or an Animal) Today and This Is What Happened To Him/Her." Each student will have two minutes or less to come up with an idea. Before continuing, make sure that everyone has selected a specific person (or animal) and event.

Next, ask students to identify the time frame that the snapshot represents. Share the examples below. Time frames are indicated in parentheses.

> *When I got on the bus, I saw my little sister standing behind the screen door. She was crying.* (about 2 minutes)

> *As I ran out the door to go to school, my dog squeezed through the door and blasted outside. I had to chase her and get her back in.* (about 3 minutes)

If you think your students would benefit from additional examples, you can use those on page 92. You might also ask a few students to share their own ideas with the class and to explain how they arrived at their time estimates. If some students feel they need to adjust their time frames after these examples, allow them to do so.

3 Debrief with students by asking, "What have you learned about selecting a topic?" (Students might say, "I didn't know that such a small thing that happened could make a story." "I didn't know I could write about something as common as the things that happen to me each day.")

Planning

4 Next, place students in pairs that you feel will make constructive duos. Have each pair choose who will be the coach first. Tell students that each coaching session will last from three to four minutes. You will keep time and then call for the pair to switch roles. The coach will ask Questions 1 through 8 on the Lesson 5 Study Sheet.

5 Remind students that you will be observing and listening to coaching sessions. Suggest that if a pair finishes too quickly—before three minutes have passed—it is clear that the coach and writer are not taking enough time to *think and talk through* each component. Explain that you are listening for a coaching round in which the coach listens carefully and encourages the writer to add more to a component. Let students know that after the first round, you will be asking one pair to model for the class.

6 When students have completed the first round, ask the selected pair to model their dialogue. Have other students identify the things the coach did or said that helped the writer. Repeat this same process after the second round.

7 After both rounds have been completed, call attention to the portion of the Lesson 5 Study Sheet called "Debrief," which consists of the following activity:

☀ The coach asks the writer: "As your writing coach, what things did I do and say that helped you?"

☀ The coach asks himself or herself: "What did I learn from the experience of being a writing coach?"

Give pairs less than one minute to debrief, calling "switch" after about 30 seconds. (Thus, each partner in a pair has about a half-minute to take each role.) Ask one pair to share their discussion.

8 Finally, explain that as you listen in on future coaching sessions, you would like to hear consistently improving rounds of coaching and debriefing. Each student should strive to become an expert writing coach, using debriefing as a way to improve and become more independent.

Drafting

9 Introduce the information from the discussion about drafting in Section 3 (see page 96). Ask students to engage in Sustained Silent Writing (SSW) for about 5–8 minutes. It's not recommended that you set a timer; most often students do write longer than the time set, but the ringing of a timer is unsettling rather than helpful. Also, for ease of rereading and revision, emphasize that students should double-space their text.

Note that the time allotments for each phase, particularly for drafting and for first revision, may seem overly brief. It's better to provide a shorter period and let students discover that they need more time than to require them to write for a lengthy amount of time. Eventually, as they become more experienced, they will be able to manage lengthier time frames independently and to control the drafting phase fluidly. (See "Drafting" on pages 97, 98, and 99, items 3, 8, and 9.)

When students begin to write, step back and allow them to work independently. The fact that students have had an opportunity to talk through the snapshot during planning makes this initial writing step more fluid, thus lowering the risk of failure. Trust that at this juncture *the experience* of writing is *the teacher*; over time the experience will provide the knowledge and confidence your students need to become more independent.

10 One minute before the appropriate time frame is up, say softly and calmly, "I can see that most of you are finished. Some still are writing. Will you finish the last sentence now and stop?"

11 Finally, debrief with your students by telling them the things you observed while they were drafting. "I noticed writers who were pausing, thinking, and then resuming writing. I also noticed writers who stopped, reread, thought, then started writing again." Remind your students that a writer is a thinker.

First Revision

12 Inform students that they are now going to do a first revision of their snapshots. This means that they are going to check for missing words. As they reread their snapshots, these questions can act as a guide: "Does my snapshot make sense? Did I leave any words out?"

13 Explain that students have 60 seconds to reread their own snapshot to locate and fix any missing words. Let them know that you will be observing their thinking behaviors as they work. Reveal that during "First Revision," the writer goes through the text word-by-word; some writers hold a finger down to each word. This is a critical process for identifying missing words. Inform your students that you will be measuring results and collecting information (data) about their success with this phase, and that it is important that each student try his or her very best. (See "First Revision," pages 99 and 100.)

Informal Publication

14 Ask for four volunteers to share their snapshots. Give all students a moment to practice. Each student's presentation should last no longer than one minute. Encourage students to give their fellow writers generous applause and to tell the writer, "I could see it when you said...." (See "Informal Publication," pages 101 and 102.)

Writing Coach's Prompt

Name _____ Date _____

DIRECTIONS: First, to help the writer narrow and focus the topic, ask Questions 1 through 4. The writer's answers should be to the point, short, and without many details. Then, ask Question 5 and listen carefully for all components and details. If the writer doesn't give enough details, use Questions 6 and 7 to get him or her to think and talk. Finally, ask Question 8.

Remember, the more the writer thinks and talks, the more fluent his or her snapshot will be.

SNAPSHOT COMPONENTS

1. Who is in your snapshot?

2. Where does your snapshot take place?

3. When does your snapshot take place?

4. What's going on? How much time does your snapshot represent?

5. Will you *talk through* your idea from its beginning to its end? Say it the way you want to write it, and I will listen very carefully to find out if you are including all components and descriptive details.

   ❑ **Who?**

Physical Features	*Personality*	*Feelings*
❑ looks/appearance?	❑ did something?	❑ tells character's feelings?
❑ clothes?	❑ said something?	
❑ approximate age?		

   ❑ **Where?**　　❑ **When?**　　❑ **What's going on?**

6a. Can you give more details about _____ ?

6b. Can you tell more details about what _____ did?

7. I heard you say _____. I didn't hear you say _____. Can you do that now?

8. Will you please *talk through* your whole snapshot again while I make a final check for each component and for descriptive details? (Make checks in the boxes in Item 5.)

DEBRIEF: Ask your partner: "As your writing coach, what things did I say and do that helped you?"
Ask yourself: "What am I learning from the experience of being a writing coach?"

MAKE A SKETCH

When your partner reads his or her snapshot aloud, sketch (on the reverse side of this paper) all of the components.

LESSON 6

A Writer Uses Interesting, Exceptional Language

PREPARING FOR THE LESSON

☀ Have available your transparency of the Lesson 5 Study Sheet, "Writing Coach's Prompt."

☀ Place a sticky-note tab on the passage from *Library Lil* excerpted in Lesson 2, page 24.

☀ Photocopy the Lesson 6 Study Sheet, "A Writer Uses Interesting, Exceptional Language" (page 41), for each student. Make an overhead transparency for your use.

☀ Identify a page from the most recent story your class has read that contains interesting and exceptional language.

Book title _____

Story title _____

Page # _____

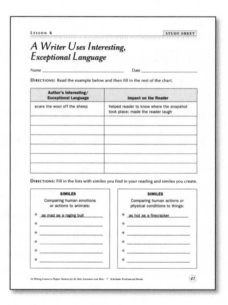

PRESENTING THE LESSON

1 Using your transparency of the Lesson 5 Study Sheet, explain that in addition to the components students have recently learned, there are three more components that make a well-crafted snapshot. The first of these will be the focus of this lesson: *a writer uses interesting, exceptional language.*

2 Review with students the snapshot components they already know by reading aloud a snapshot from the book *The Watsons Go to Birmingham—1963,* by Christopher Paul Curtis (page 39). Instruct students to use Questions 1 through 5 of the study sheet to analyze the components of the text. Hold a brief classroom discussion to cover these familiar components. (Alert students ahead of time that this snapshot contains all components except *Who,* and mention that the storyteller in this book is a young boy who is about 9 years old, named Kenny.)

The snapshot reads:

> *It was one of those super-duper-cold Saturdays. One of those days that when you breathed out, your breath kind of hung frozen in the air like a hunk of smoke and you could walk along and look exactly like a train blowing out big, fat, white puffs of smoke.*
>
> *It was so cold that if you were stupid enough to go outside your eyes would automatically blink a thousand times all by themselves, probably so the juice inside of them wouldn't freeze up. It was so cold that if you spit, the slob would be an ice cube before it hit the ground. It was about a zillion degrees below zero.*
>
> (Christopher Paul Curtis, 1995 p. 1)

3 Reread the passage from *Library Lil* (page 24), and remind students how Williams used interesting and exceptional language like *scare the wool off the sheep*. Point out that "she knows how to use *rich descriptions and make actions clear and vivid*." (The italicized words come from the Indiana writing rubric. Insert or paraphrase the words from your own state's rubric.) Emphasize that Williams knows how to select precise words that have an impact on a reader.

4 Give each student a copy of the Lesson 6 Study Sheet, "A Writer Uses Interesting and Exceptional Language." Use your transparency to point out such language in the above example from *Library Lil,* which is already filled in. Inform students that you are going to read aloud Curtis' snapshot again, and that this time they should focus on the language. Ask them to listen extra carefully for the author's use of interesting, exceptional language. Remind them to be prepared to give examples. After reading, write the first student example on the transparency. Read it to the class and have students write more examples. Finally, ask students to share their findings; write them in on the transparency. For example, *exaggeration* to convey humor is used frequently:

*   *super-duper-cold Saturdays*

*   *eyes automatically blink a thousand times all by themselves*

*   *about a zillion degrees below zero*

5 Encourage students to think of one way in which they might be able to increase their awareness of interesting language in text. If necessary, help to elicit the idea that simply reading good writing, especially reading it with a tuned-in ear for language, is one of the best ways. Place each student with a partner. Have students find the page in the literature book that you have already identified. Ask each pair of students to scan the page to find examples of interesting and exceptional language, write down the information on the chart, and then share it with the class.

6 Ask students if they can recall the name for the language structure that uses "like" to compare one thing to another. (Many will probably be able to identify it as a *simile*.) Explain that this is another effective way for an author to use interesting and exceptional

language. Invite students to find Curtis' similes (*like a hunk of smoke; like a train blowing out big, fat, white puffs of smoke*). Ask students to explain why words like these interest and fascinate readers.

7 Discuss the first example in the *simile* section of the study sheet. Ask students to brainstorm some interesting similes they know, and then continue to fill in the lists. Encourage them to tap into their own imaginations to come up with original similes. (A second grader came up with this one: *as scared as a bat during the day,* and a fifth-grader thought up this: *the man snored like a broken-down car.*)

8 After students have filled in the study sheet, make large charts of the lists and post them in your classroom. Leave room for additions and invite students to add to the lists as they find similes while reading or as they think of original ones. When the lists are full, type them up and photocopy them so students can place a copy inside their writing journals. You might enhance this lesson by assembling all the lists within one booklet and publishing your own classroom book of similes. You could also add a mini-lesson on metaphors and continue building that list.

A Writer Uses Interesting, Exceptional Language

Name _____   Date _____

DIRECTIONS: Read the example below and then fill in the rest of the chart.

Author's Interesting/ Exceptional Language	Impact on the Reader
scare the wool off the sheep	helped reader to know where the snapshot took place; made the reader laugh

DIRECTIONS: Fill in the lists with similes you find in your reading and similes you create.

SIMILES	SIMILES
Comparing human emotions or actions to animals:	Comparing human actions or physical conditions to things:

SIMILES

Comparing human emotions
or actions to animals:

☀ as mad as a raging bull _____

☀ _____

☀ _____

☀ _____

☀ _____

☀ _____

SIMILES

Comparing human actions or
physical conditions to things:

☀ as hot as a firecracker _____

☀ _____

☀ _____

☀ _____

☀ _____

☀ _____

A Writer Includes a Dynamic Beginning

PREPARING FOR THE LESSON

☀ Have available the read-aloud excerpt from Curtis' book, *The Watsons Go to Birmingham—1963* (Lesson 6, page 39).

☀ Make a copy of the Lesson 7 Study Sheet, "A Writer Includes a Dynamic Beginning," (page 44) for each student.

☀ Identify and select two or three stories from the class reader, literature anthology, or a novel that your students are currently reading (or have recently read) that model a snapshot with a dynamic beginning. Snapshots may come from the beginning paragraph of the story or from within the story.

Book title _____ Story title _____ Page # _____

Book title _____ Story title _____ Page # _____

Book title _____ Story title _____ Page # _____

PRESENTING THE LESSON

1 Read aloud Curtis' first two sentences (which are essentially one long sentence broken into two parts):

> *It was one of those super-duper-cold Saturdays. One of those days that when you breathed out, your breath kind of hung frozen in the air like a hunk of smoke and you could walk along and look exactly like a train blowing out big, fat, white puffs of smoke.*

Ask students, "What do you feel when you hear Curtis' first sentence?" After their responses, follow up with a question like, "What does a writer intend for the first sentence to do to a reader?" (The first sentence should get the reader's attention. It should draw the reader in so that he or she wants to read further.) Explain that a dynamic first sentence is one of the components of a well-crafted snapshot. Authors deliberately and carefully craft a first sentence.

2   Have students open their books to the first story you have selected and analyze the author's dynamic beginning. What language choices has the author deliberately made? Ask students to fill out the first row on the Lesson 7 Study Sheet, then read the other selections and continue to fill out the chart. (Remember that your snapshot choices do not always have to come from the beginning of a story or chapter. Often a brief snapshot within a larger section will contain its own dynamic beginning.)

3   Pair students up. Have each pair browse through the books to find at least one more example of a dynamic beginning. Students should then jot down the information on a chart. When all have finished, invite the pairs to share their discoveries and analyses with the rest of the class.

4   During classroom reading instruction, continue to help students think about how an author writes a dynamic beginning. Suggest that they record examples of dynamic beginnings in their literature logs or journals as they read new assignments. Recommend that they use the format of the Lesson 7 Study Sheet.

A Writer Includes a Dynamic Beginning

Name _____   Date _____

DIRECTIONS: First, listen as your teacher reads aloud some snapshots, and fill in each column. Then, with your partner, find additional snapshots that have a dynamic beginning and fill in each column.

Title/Page #/ Paragraph #	Dynamic Beginning Sentence of This Snapshot	What Is It About the Author's Language Choices That Draws the Reader In?
	_____ _____ _____	_____ _____ _____
	_____ _____ _____	_____ _____ _____
	_____ _____ _____	_____ _____ _____
	_____ _____ _____	_____ _____ _____

A Writer Includes a Tie-Up Ending

PREPARING FOR THE LESSON

☀ Make a copy of the Lesson 8 Study Sheet, "A Writer Includes a Tie-Up Ending" (page 47) for each student and make a transparency for your own use.

PRESENTING THE LESSON

1 Tell students that you are going to twice read aloud a short story, "The Lazy Miner." The first time you will leave off the ending and the second time you will finish the story. After the first reading, ask students to describe what it feels like when the writer leaves the reader dangling without the closure of a tie-up ending. After the second reading, ask students to identify the writer's tie-up ending.

LESSON 8 STUDY SHEET

A Writer Includes a Tie-Up Ending

Name _____ Date _____

DIRECTIONS: Read the snapshot that follows. How did the author create a tie-up ending? Does the ending make you, the reader, feel like the text has closure? Discuss your ideas with your class.

This drizzly morning as our school bus was stopped at a light, I noticed an old man walking on the sidewalk. He had on a tattered black coat and a shabby looking black knit cap that was pulled down tight over his forehead. His face was unshaved and his eyes had dark rings around them like shadows on a moonlit night. His ragged pants hung down from under his coat, and I could see holes in the toes of his shoes. His shoulders were hunched forward, and he sort of stumbled along. Was he going to fall into the street? Then our bus lurched forward and sped on down the street. I wanted to scream, "Stop! Let me out!" But, I didn't say anything.

—Sidney (Grade 5)

DIRECTIONS: Think of ways you can make a good tie-up ending. Jot down your ideas on this chart.

Possible Ways to Create a Tie-Up Ending

DIRECTIONS: Write a new tie-up ending for Sidney's snapshot.

_____

_____

_____

16 Writing Lessons to Prepare Students for the State Assessment and More • Scholastic Professional Books 47

The Lazy Miner

Long ago, during the gold rush days the waters of some western rivers and streams were said to be full of gold. Hoping to get rich without working very hard, hundreds of people traveled out West to pan for gold. Scooping up mud and gravel from the streams, they would shake the wet earth and rocks through a sieve, looking for the little nuggets of gold that were said to be mixed in with the soil. As the people worked, they would tell tales about the wonderful things they'd seen.

One famous story was about a miner who was too lazy to wash his long underwear. Instead, he decided to save himself the work of scrubbing by tying the long underwear to a limb that hung over a little stream and letting it dangle in the water. He figured that the rushing water would wash it for him. Well, one morning the miner was too lazy even to get up and pan for gold. As a matter of fact, he was so lazy that for an entire week, the underwear just hung there and was washed by the water rushing through it.

Finally, the miner got up and remembered his long underwear. He went to fish it out and what do you think he found? His underwear was gold plated!

(From *One-Minute Bedtime Stories*, Shari Lewis with Lan O'Kun. Doubleday and Company, 1982.)

2 Remind students that snapshots can be found anywhere in a text—in the beginning, middle, or near the end—and may not have the same tie-up ending that the kind of snapshot they are currently writing requires. Underscore that the kind of snapshot they are working on now is like a very short, stand-alone story, and therefore it needs a tie-up ending. Like short story writers, snapshot writers include a tie-up ending because they do not want to leave the reader dangling. A good ending provides a sense of closure for the reader.

3 Ask your students to read the snapshot on the Lesson 8 Study Sheet. Discuss how the author created a tie-up ending. (In the last two sentences the author brought closure by writing a statement and a quotation that connected to the first sentence.)

> *This drizzly morning as our school bus was stopped at a light, I noticed an old man walking on the sidewalk. He had on a tattered black coat and a shabby looking black knit cap that was pulled down tight over his forehead. His face was unshaved and his eyes had dark rings around them like shadows on a moonlit night. His ragged pants hung down from under his coat, and I could see holes in the toes of his shoes. His shoulders were hunched forward, and he sort of stumbled along. Was he going to fall into the street? Then our bus lurched forward and sped on down the street. I wanted to scream, "Stop! Let me out!" But, I didn't say anything.*
>
> —Sidney (Grade 5)

4 Invite your students to brainstorm ideas that can be used as guidelines for creating a tie-up ending. To start their thinking, write on the chalkboard one of the ideas listed below. Add students' ideas as they volunteer them. Tell students to jot down all the possibilities in the chart on their study sheet.

> *Write a statement that connects with your first sentence.*
>
> *Write a quotation that connects with your first sentence.*
>
> *Write something that the main character does or says that brings the action to a close.*
>
> *Write a question that causes a reader to think about something that might happen to the main character next. (In other words, deliberately write a cliff-hanger.)*

(Sometimes a writer will purposefully craft a cliff-hanger ending to tie into the story's plot and character development. This type of ending is very different from a carelessly constructed ending that just leaves the reader dangling.)

5 Have students remove Sidney's last two sentences and brainstorm other ways that she could have written a tie-up ending.

A Writer Includes a Tie-Up Ending

Name _____ Date _____

DIRECTIONS: Read the snapshot that follows. How did the author create a tie-up ending? Does the ending make you, the reader, feel like the text has closure? Discuss your ideas with your class.

> This drizzly morning as our school bus was stopped at a light, I noticed an old man walking on the sidewalk. He had on a tattered black coat and a shabby looking black knit cap that was pulled down tight over his forehead. His face was unshaved and his eyes had dark rings around them like shadows on a moonlit night. His ragged pants hung down from under his coat, and I could see holes in the toes of his shoes. His shoulders were hunched forward, and he sort of stumbled along. Was he going to fall into the street? Then our bus lurched forward and sped on down the street. I wanted to scream, "Stop! Let me out!" But, I didn't say anything.
>
> —Sidney (Grade 5)

DIRECTIONS: Think of ways you can make a good tie-up ending. Jot down your ideas on this chart.

Possible Ways to Create a Tie-Up Ending

DIRECTIONS: Write a new tie-up ending for Sidney's snapshot.

_____

_____

_____

Debriefing to Become Better and Better

PREPARING FOR THE LESSON

☀ Have available the transparency of the Lesson 5 Study Sheet, "Writing Coach's Prompt," (page 37).

☀ Photocopy for each student the Lesson 9 Study Sheet, "A Writing Coach's Listening Skills" (page 50). Make a transparency for your use.

☀ Read the chart, the "Writing Coach's Evaluation Checklist of Snapshot Skills," on page 95. Refer to your state's standards in the category of listening and speaking. If you find a skill from the standards that is not included on the checklist, be sure to add it.

☀ Make a transparency of the "Writing Coach's Evaluation Checklist of Snapshot Skills" chart that includes any changes you have made.

PRESENTING THE LESSON

Debriefing

1 Remind students that during the next few weeks, they are striving to achieve two competencies—becoming highly-skilled snapshot writers *and* highly-skilled snapshot writing coaches. Each time they coach a writer, the goal is for their coaching skills to improve.

But how do people get better at what they do? Invite students to offer their own ideas on this subject. Hold a class discussion. To help students focus, suggest that they think of a skill that they have learned over time—perhaps a sport, a musical instrument, or a dance. They will undoubtedly mention "practice"; but help move the discussion in a direction that elicits the ideas of *reflection* and *analysis*. Doing something well involves the strategy of thinking about (reflecting) and figuring out (analyzing) what one is learning from an experience. The process of thinking about one's thinking is called *metacognition*. Debriefing is a device used by many prople to reflect and improve. For example, professionals use it as a way to get better at the tasks in their jobs.

Using your transparency of the Lesson 5 Study Sheet, "Writing Coach's Prompt," highlight the row called "Debrief." Remind students that each time they think about the experience of being a writing coach and figure out what they are learning about this role, they are engaging in debriefing. This analysis will help them to become better coaches; it is an effective way to improve (streamline) coaching skills.

Then, be sure to ask students to think about and share responses to the question: "What am I learning from the experience of being a writing coach?" Their responses might include:

☀ *I am learning that I have to be a good listener.*

☀ *I am learning that I have to know the snapshot components.*

2 Focus on the skill of listening and have students determine what a good listener does and says. Using the Lesson 9 Study Sheet, "A Writing Coach's Listening Skills," ask students to brainstorm a list of good listening skills. Some possible skills are listed below. This is only a partial list, and students should be encouraged to think of other skills to include on their study sheets. This will be an ongoing process, as the study sheet explains. It may span several days or weeks. Each time students list a new skill, they should date its entry on the study sheet. This will allow them to record their progress.

Things a Skilled Listener Does...	Things a Skilled Listener Says...
makes and keeps eye contact	not much
makes the writer feel he/she has full attention—for example, leaning toward the writer	"Will you please repeat what you just said?'
	paraphrases using the writer's words only: "So, you said..."

3 After you and the students have listed some listening skills, ask two students to model each skill. For example, ask a pair to show what a coach does when he or she is giving the writer full attention. What are some of the coach's specific actions? How might the writer respond?

4 Point out the last section of the study sheet, "Ongoing Debriefing." This is a critical part of the learning process. Explain that it is a self-analysis chart designed for their own use, and that there is no "right" or "wrong" here. After a coaching session, each student should step back and analyze his or her own performance, using the rating system on the study sheet. Over time, this will help students become better coaches and get better at debriefing.

5 Place your transparency of the "Writing Coach's Evaluation Checklist of Snapshot Skills" on the overhead and highlight the row that says, "listens attentively." Be sure students realize that developing good listening skills is only one of a number of key coaching skills. Inform them that during the writing of their second snapshot, you will be walking around the room, observing the sessions, and that during all snapshots thereafter, you will be collecting and reporting data about each coach's skills. As students become more experienced, you will also be looking for other key coaching skills on the checklist—for example, "supports with positive, constructive comments" or "probes to get more details." Make clear to students that each of the skills on the checklist is important.

A Writing Coach's Listening Skills

Name _____   Date _____

DIRECTIONS: A writing coach is a skilled listener. Brainstorm a list of the things you think a skilled listener does and says. Fill in the first entries with your teacher during the lesson.

As you become a better writing coach, add new skills to this list. Ask yourself the following question: "What more am I finding out about being a skilled listener?" Write the skill(s) on the list and jot down the date beside the skill (such as 10/10/200__).

Things a Skilled Listener Does	Date	Things A Skilled Listener Says	Date

ONGOING DEBRIEFING

DIRECTIONS: After a coaching session, think about and rate your own listening skills as follows:

    5 = Top Notch   **3 = Middle of the Road**   **1 = Needs Improvement**

Repeat this process on several different dates.

Date/Rating	Things I Did and/or Said

Fine Tuning Coaching Skills

PREPARING FOR THE LESSON

☀ Make a copy of the "Teacher's Snapshot Script" on page 53 for each student. You might choose to use the model snapshot included on the study sheet or use the one you wrote for Lesson 4.

☀ Have available the transparency of the "Phases of the Writing Process" diagram (original on page 91).

☀ Have available the transparency of the "Writing Coach's Evaluation Checklist of Snapshot Skills" (page 95).

☀ Read and review the "Planning" subsection of Section 3 (pages 93 to 94).

PRESENTING THE LESSON

1 Highlight the planning phase on your transparency, "Phases of the Writing Process." Inform students that you are going to model another coaching session, using the same snapshot modeled in Lesson 4. This time, however, the new components—exceptional word usage, dynamic beginning, and tie-up ending—will now be added to your snapshot. As in Lesson 4, you will be the writer and the students will take on the role of writing coach. Emphasize that it is the coach's responsibility to ask questions, listen very carefully, and get the writer to talk a lot more than the coach.

2 Give each student a copy of the "Teacher's Snapshot Script" and ask them to fold the page so that the only portion visible is the snapshot components list.

Remind students that during the modeling session in Lesson 4, you paused often to show visible signs of thinking. This is called "mulling"—a writer's thinking, pondering, and deliberating. Because your students may still think that ideas come to a writer's mind quickly and automatically, you should stress that a writer frequently is uncertain about how to express an idea and uses thinking and problem solving, or mulling, to put an idea into words. It is such an important part of writing, that the coach needs to know how to encourage the writer to mull ideas over. Make students aware that during this modeling session, you are going to teach coaches how to get the writer to mull over ideas and word choices.

3 Ask students to look at each of the questions listed as "Snapshot Components." Tell them that the most effective way for the coach to get the writer to *talk and think through* each

component is to break the questions into natural chunks or groups. Advise them to use the following groupings as they ask you the questions. (You can follow the "Snapshot Text" for your answers as you model the process.)

- ☀ Questions 1 through 4 make up the first grouping. These questions help the writer narrow and focus the topic. They are aimed at eliciting answers that are short, to the point, and without any details.

- ☀ Question 5 is next; coaches need to listen carefully for all components and details. If the writer doesn't give enough details, Questions 6 and 7 should be used to get the writer to think and talk.

- ☀ Questions 8 and 9 get the writer to think about a dynamic beginning and a tie-up ending.

- ☀ Finally, Question 10 provides an opportunity to review everything.

4 After you have completed Question 10 on the "Teacher's Snapshot Script," ask your students to identify something you did that showed you were mulling over ideas. For example, for Questions 7a, 9, and 10, you might have said:

"Mmmmm, I think I'll say, 'As usual, he was dressed for work looking as neat as a groom on his wedding day.'"

"I'm not sure how I felt. I'll have to think about this some more."

"I need more time to think about this. I'll have to give this some more thought."

Ask students what they think is going on in the writer's mind during the mulling over stages. Help them to see that when a writer is thinking about how to construct the text, he or she may know in general how to express the idea, but may not know the exact words to use. Place your transparency of the "Writing Coach's Evaluation Checklist of Snapshot Skills" on the overhead and call attention to this skill.

5 Next, highlight on that same transparency the row that says, "gets writer to talk a lot." Tell students that the basic rule of coaching is this: "The writer talks a lot—the coach prompts the writer's thinking and talking." The more the writer talks, the better organized and more fluent his or her snapshot will be.

Let students know that you will be observing them during the planning phase of the next snapshot. You'll be listening to hear if coaches:

- ☀ know all the components

- ☀ get the writer to talk a lot

6 Finally, on the Lesson 11 Study Sheet, "Writing Coach's Prompt," focus attention on the part called "Debrief." Ask students something like, "So, what are you learning from being a writing coach?" (Responses may include: *"I must be a good listener." "I have to know the components." "I have to get the writer to talk more." "I have to try harder to get the writer to mull over ideas."*)

SNAPSHOT COMPONENTS	SNAPSHOT TEXT
1. Who is in your snapshot?	...my husband
2. Where does your snapshot take place?	...in the kitchen
3. When does your snapshot take place?	...this morning
4. What's going on? How much time does this snapshot represent?	...He is cooking his breakfast and talking to me. ...about 2 minutes or less
5. Talk through your idea from its beginning to its end. Say it the way you want to write it, and I will listen very carefully to find out if you are including all components and descriptive details. ☐ **Who?** *Physical Features*　*Personality*　*Feelings* ☐ looks/ 　　☐ did 　　☐ tells 　 appearance? 　 something? 　 character's ☐ clothes? 　☐ said 　　　 feelings? ☐ approx. age? 　 something? ☐ **Where?**　☐ **When?**　☐ **What's going on?** ☐ **Uses exceptional/interesting language?** ☐ **Dynamic beginning?**　☐ **Tie-up ending?**	This morning my husband stood in front of the stove cooking his eggs. He said, "I wish someone would cook my breakfast for me." Then he looked at me and said, "But I know how busy you are. You don't need one more thing to do!"
6a. Can you give more details about *Who?*	This morning my husband, tall and handsome, stood in front of the stove cooking his eggs. He said, "I wish someone would cook my breakfast for me." Then he looked at me and said, "But I know how busy you are. You don't need one more thing to do!"
6b. Can you tell more details about what he did?	He yawned and stretched and said, "I wish someone would cook my breakfast for me."
7a. I heard you say _____, but I didn't hear you say how he felt. Can you do that now?	Yes, he was really feeling sorry for himself. I think I'll say: He yawned and stretched and whined in a self-pitying voice, "Gosh, I wish someone would cook my breakfast for me!"
7b. Are you sure you used enough exceptional language? (Coach goes back to Item 7a because writer needs to put more exceptional language in text.)	Ahhhhh, if I say, "dressed for work looking as neat as a groom on his wedding day," then I've used a simile. Sooo, I think I'll say, "As usual, he was dressed for work looking as neat as a groom on his wedding day."

SNAPSHOT COMPONENTS	SNAPSHOT TEXT
8. Can you make a more dynamic beginning? One that will get your reader's attention?	*Yes, I think I'll add more description, maybe about how he was dressed. He is always dressed so neatly!*
9. How do you plan to tie-up the ending?	*Something about him looking at me and smiling before he speaks. Then, I'll tell how his smile and maybe his look made me feel— maybe like a lucky wife or something. I'm not sure how I did feel. I'll have to think about this some more.*
10. Will you please talk your whole snapshot through again while I make a final check for each component and for descriptive details? (Mark the checklist in Item 5.)	*This morning my husband, tall and handsome, stood in front of the stove cooking his eggs. As usual, he was dressed for work looking as neat as a groom on his wedding day. He yawned and stretched and whined in a self-pitying voice, "Gosh, I wish someone would cook my breakfast for me." Then, he looked at me and said, "But I know how busy you are. You don't need one more thing to do!"* *I'm not quite sure how I'm going to end my snapshot yet. I think I want to say something about how I felt, but I need more time to think it over. Maybe I felt like a lucky woman, maybe accomplished. I will have to give it some more thought.*

LESSON 11

Writing the Second Snapshot

PREPARING FOR THE LESSON

☀ Photocopy for each student the Lesson 11 Study Sheet, "Writing Coach's Prompt" (page 58). Make a transparency of this same study sheet for your use.

☀ Have your transparency of the "Phases of the Writing Process" diagram (page 91) ready.

☀ Read and review the following background material: "Selecting a Topic," "Planning," "Drafting," "First Revision," and "Informal Publication" (pages 90 to 101 of Section 3).

PRESENTING THE LESSON

Selecting a Topic

1 Tell students that it's their turn to plan and write their own second snapshot. Highlight "Selecting a Topic" on your transparency of "Phases of the Writing Process."

2 Let students know that they will be using the same general topic that they used for their first snapshot—"I Saw Someone (or an Animal) Today and This Is What Happened to Him/Her." Each student will have two minutes or less to come up with an idea. Check to make sure that everyone has selected a specific topic. Next, ask students to identify the time frame that the snapshot represents. Ask a few students to share their ideas; make certain that each of these represents a short span of time. If some students need to adjust their topics or time frames, encourage them to do so.

Planning

3 Next, arrange students in pairs you feel will be constructive. Have each pair choose who will be coach first. Tell students that each coaching session will last from four to five minutes. You will keep the time and then call for the pair to switch roles. The coach will ask Questions 1–10 from the Lesson 11 Study Sheet.

4 Remind students that you will be observing and listening to coaching sessions. Alert them that if you notice a pair who finishes too quickly—in under four minutes—it will be clear that the coach and writer are not taking enough time to *think and talk through* each component. Explain that you are listening for a coaching round in which the coach listens carefully and encourages the writer to add more to a component. After the first round, ask one pair to model for the class.

5 After you have selected a pair, explain that this coaching session will act as a debriefing session for the whole class. While students listen to this coaching session, they should be asking themselves the following questions:

> *What did I see or hear that told me the coach knows all of the components?*
>
> *What did the coach say and do to model good listening skills?*
>
> *How did the coach get the writer to talk a lot?*
>
> *How did the coach get the writer to mull over his or her thinking?*

After the coaching session, conduct a whole-class discussion.

6 Then, tell students to switch roles. Let them know that they will also have five minutes for this second round. Observe and listen to pairs.

7 Invite each pair to debrief. Read the following questions aloud, and have the writer answer each question. Encourage the writer to address the writing coach directly as he or she speaks.

> *What did you see or hear that told you the coach knows all of the components?*
>
> *What did the coach say and do to model good listening skills?*
>
> *How did the coach get you to talk a lot?*
>
> *How did the coach get you to mull over your thinking?*

8 Finally, explain that as you listen in to future coaching sessions, you would like to hear consistently improving rounds of coaching and debriefing. Each student should strive to become an expert writing coach and an expert writer, using debriefing as a way to improve and become more independent.

Drafting

9 Discuss with your students the background information about drafting (located in Section 3) and highlight this phase on your transparency of "Phases of the Writing Process."

Re-emphasize that you want them to double-space their text. Ask them to select an appropriate time to engage in Sustained Silent Writing (SSW). Extend the time choice so that it now runs from 15 to 20 minutes. Explain that if the planning sessions have gone well, each writer needs a minimum of 15 minutes to write a well-crafted snapshot.

When students begin to write, step back and allow them to work independently. The fact that students have had an opportunity to talk through the snapshot makes this initial writing step more fluid, thus lowering the risk of failure. Remember that the experience of writing *is itself the teacher.* Trust that the students' experience of writing their first snapshot has given them knowledge and confidence, enabling them to work more independently. As they write, observe students to see if they are:

pausing, thinking, and mulling over an idea, then resuming writing

rereading and making changes to the content of the text

using the entire time, and still feeling they could use more time

10 One minute before the appropriate time frame is up, softly and calmly say, "I can see that most of you are finished. Some are still writing. Will you finish your last sentence now?"

Debrief with your students by telling them the things you observed while they were drafting. Refer to Item 10 on the study sheet and offer a reinforcing statement, such as, "I noticed writers who were pausing, thinking, and mulling over an idea, then resuming writing." Ask students to do a self-check by using the list in Item 10 to do a quick review of their snapshots. Allow a few minutes for them to do this. Finally, remind them that a writer is a thinker who mulls over ideas and a problem solver who makes large and small decisions.

First Revision

11 Highlight the First Revision phase on your "Phases of the Writing Process" transparency. Tell students that they are now going to do a first revision of their snapshots. This means that they are going to check for missing words. As they reread their snapshots, these questions can act as a guide: "Does my snapshot make sense? Did I leave any words out?"

Explain that they have two minutes, to reread their own snapshot to locate and fix any missing words. Let them know that you will be observing their thinking behaviors as they work. Remind them that during "First Revision," the writer goes through the text word by word. This is a critical step for catching errors. Reiterate that when they write their third snapshot, you will be collecting information and making evaluations about their success with this phase, and that it is important that each student try his or her very best.

Informal Publication

12 Highlight the Informal Publication phase on your "Phases of the Writing Process" transparency. Ask for four volunteers who wish to share their snapshots and give the students a moment to practice. Each student's sharing should last about one minute. Encourage the class to give their fellow writers generous applause. Encourage students to offer the writer feedback that is specific and detailed. They might, for instance, tell the writer: "I could see it when you said...."

Writing Coach's Prompt

Name _____   Date _____

DIRECTIONS: First, to help the writer narrow and focus the topic, ask Questions 1 through 4. The writer's answers should be to the point, short, and without any details. Then, ask Question 5 and listen carefully for all components and details. If the writer doesn't give enough details, use Questions 6 and 7 to get him or her to think and talk. Ask questions 8 and 9 so the writer will think about the dynamic beginning and tie-up ending. Finally, ask question 10.

SNAPSHOT COMPONENTS

1. Who is in your snapshot?

2. Where does your snapshot take place?

3. When does your snapshot take place?

4. What's going on? How much time does your snapshot represent?

5. Will you talk through your idea from its beginning to its end? Say it the way you want to write it, and I will listen very carefully to find out if you are including all components and descriptive details.

     ❑ **Who?**

Physical Features	*Personality*	*Feelings*
❑ looks/appearance?	❑ did something?	❑ tells character's feelings?
❑ clothes?	❑ said something?	
❑ approximate age?		

     ❑ **Where?**   ❑ **When?**   ❑ **What's going on?**

     ❑ **Uses exceptional/interesting language?**

     ❑ **Uncludes dynamic beginning?**   ❑ **Includes tie-up ending?**

6. Can you give more details about _____?

7. Are you going to add some more exceptional language?

8. Does your snapshot have a dynamic beginning, one that will catch your reader's attention?

9. Does your snapshot have a tie-up ending?

10. Will you please *talk through* your whole snapshot again while I make a final check for each component and for descriptive details? (Make checks in the boxes in Item 5.)

DEBRIEF: Ask your partner: "What things did I say and do that helped you?"
Ask yourself: "What am I learning from the experience of being a writing coach?"

MAKE A SKETCH:

When your partner reads his or her snapshot, sketch (on the reverse side of this paper) all of the components.

Editing for Capitalization and Spelling

PREPARING FOR THE LESSON

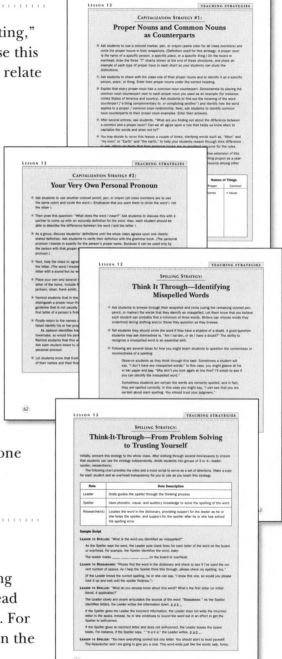

☀ Read and review the following material: the "Editing," discussion on pages 106–108 of Section 3. Because this material is a series of teaching steps and tips that relate directly to this lesson, you may wish to make a photocopy of the information and keep it handy.

☀ Have available your transparency of the "Phases of the Writing Process" diagram (see page 91).

☀ Review and have available the "Capitalization Strategy #1: Proper Nouns and Common Nouns as Counterparts" and "Capitalization Strategy #2: Your Very Own Personal Pronoun," that follow on pages 61–62. You'll also want to review and have available the "Spelling Strategy: Think-It-Through—Identifying Misspelled Words," and the "Spelling Strategy: Think-It-Through—From Problem Solving to Trusting Yourself," on pages 63–65.

☀ Assemble different colored marking pens or pencils, one for each capitalization strategy and one for spelling.

PRESENTING THE LESSON

Editing

1 Highlight "Editing" on your "Phases of the Writing Process" transparency. Have different students read aloud the five editing tasks listed on the diagram. For each task, add further details from the same list in the Editing subsection on page 104.

2 Let students know that they will be focusing on two capitalization strategies and on a spelling strategy. (In a later lesson, you will ask them to focus further on capitalization and on punctuation.) Explain that they will work through one strategy at a time because it is much easier to learn the strategies this way. Eventually, with more practice, the strategies will probably become automatic, and students should be able to apply several at one time.

3　Students will be using their second snapshot to edit for capital letters. Ask each student to get a colored pen or pencil and follow the directions for "Capitalization Strategy # 1: Proper Nouns and Common Nouns as Counterparts."

4　Repeat Step 3, this time using "Capitalization Strategy #2, Your Very Own Personal Pronoun." Distribute a different colored pen or pencil to students.

5　Remind students that they will also use their second snapshot to edit for spelling. This time, instruct them to work with the remaining colored pen or pencil, so that their corrections for different kinds of capitalization and those for spelling will all be distinguishable. Follow the directions for "Spelling Strategy: Think It Through—Identifying Misspelled Words." After students have identified misspelled words, continue by using "Spelling Strategy: Think-It-Through—From Problem Solving to Trusting Yourself." This sequence of spelling strategies can be used during this lesson and also during Lesson 16.

6　After teaching all strategies, invite students to debrief. For example, you might ask students, "How does a writer use capital letters to convey meaning to a reader?" and "How do you think the Think-It-Through strategies will help you to be a better speller?"

CAPITALIZATION STRATEGY #1:

Proper Nouns and Common Nouns as Counterparts

☀ Ask students to use a colored marker, pen, or crayon (same color for all class members) and circle the *proper nouns* in their snapshots. (Definition used for this strategy: *A proper noun is the name of a specific person, a specific place, or a specific thing.*) On the board or overhead, draw the three "T" charts shown at the end of these directions, and place an example of each type of proper noun in each chart so your students can study the distinctions.

☀ Ask students to share with the class one of their proper nouns and to identify it as a specific person, place, or thing. Enter their proper nouns under the correct heading.

☀ Explain that every proper noun has a *common noun* counterpart. Demonstrate by placing the common noun counterpart next to each proper noun you used as an example (for instance: United States of America and country). Ask students to find out the meaning of the word *counterpart* ("a thing complementary to, or completing another") and identify how the word applies to a proper/common noun relationship. Next, ask students to identify common noun counterparts to their proper noun examples. Enter their answers.

☀ After several entries, ask students, "What are you finding out about the difference between a common and a proper noun? Can we all agree upon a rule that helps us know when to capitalize the words and when not to?"

☀ You may decide to rerun this lesson a couple of times, clarifying words such as, "Mom" and "my mom" or "Earth" and "the earth," to help your students reason through their difference in use. Inform students that their grammar books are an excellent resource for the rules.

☀ Engaging your class in the writing of a class grammar book is an effective extension of this and other strategies in this book. Many teachers use this authentic writing project as a year-long inquiry, publishing a class-made grammar book that becomes a resource among other published grammar texts.

Names of Persons		Names of Places		Names of Things	
Proper	Common	Proper	Common	Proper	Common
• Lynn Smith	• woman	• College Park Cinema	• movie theater	• Kleenex	• tissue

CAPITALIZATION STRATEGY #2:

Your Very Own Personal Pronoun

☀ Ask students to use another colored pencil, pen, or crayon (all class members are to use the same color) and circle the word *I*. Emphasize that you want them to circle the *word I*, not the *letter i.*

☀ Then pose this question: "What does the word *I* mean?" Ask students to discuss this with a partner to come up with an accurate definition for the word. Also, each student should be able to describe the difference between the word *I* and the letter *i.*

☀ As a group, discuss students' definitions until the whole class agrees upon one clearly-stated definition. Ask students to verify their definition with the grammar book. (The personal pronoun *I* stands in exactly for the person's proper name. Because it can be used only by the person with that proper name, it could be called each person's very own personal pronoun.)

☀ Next, help the class to agree upon a follow-up statement that distinguishes the word from the letter. (The *word I* means the same thing as a person's name. The letter *i* is an alphabet letter with a sound but no word meaning.)

☀ Place your own and several students' names on the board and do not capitalize the first letter of the name. Include first names, first and last names, and titles: mrs. hanover, jackson, oliver, frank smith, jessica sanders.

☀ Remind students that in the English language the use of a capital letter serves to distinguish a proper noun from a common noun. Then discuss with them another usage guideline that is not usually found in the grammar books. The use of a capital letter as the first letter of a person's first, middle, and last name is an expression of respect.

☀ Finally return to the names on the board. Point to your own name. Then have each student listed identify his or her proper noun.

As Jackson identifies his, write *jackson = i*. Point out that if Jackson's name were lowercase, so would his personal pronoun be lowercase. Repeat the same for the others. Remind students that this would not only be incorrect, it could be seen to be disrespectful. Ask each student listed to come to the chalkboard to correct his or her proper noun and personal pronoun.

☀ Let students know that from now oxn, you will expect them to edit for correct capitalization of their names and their first person personal pronoun (*I*).

SPELLING STRATEGY:

Think-It-Through—Identifying Misspelled Words

☀ Ask students to browse through their snapshot and circle (using the remaining colored pen, pencil, or marker) the words that they identify as misspelled. Let them know that you believe each student can probably find a minimum of three words. Writers can choose words they underlined during drafting and/or those they question as they browse.

☀ Tell students they should circle the word if they have a shadow of a doubt. A good question students may ask themselves is, "Am I certain, or do I have a doubt?" The ability to recognize a misspelled word is an essential skill.

☀ Following are several ideas for how you might teach students to question the correctness or incorrectness of a spelling:

- Observe students as they think through this task. Sometimes a student will say, "I don't have any misspelled words!" In this case, you might glance at his or her paper and say, "Why don't you look again at line five? I'll watch to see if you can identify the misspelled word."

- Sometimes students are certain the words are correctly spelled, and in fact, they *are* spelled correctly. In this case you might say, "I can see that you are certain about each spelling. You should trust your judgment."

- After instructing students on how to identify misspelled words, it's a good idea to gather data about their ability to do this task. Some teachers have a checklist containing students' names and use a plus (+) or a minus (–) coding system to document student skill level. Others use a rating system: 6 = finds most misspellings; 3 = finds some misspellings; 1 = finds very few misspellings.

SPELLING STRATEGY:

Think-It-Through—From Problem Solving to Trusting Yourself

Initially, present this strategy to the whole class. After working through several mini-lessons to ensure that students can use the strategy independently, divide students into groups of 3 or 4—leader, speller, researcher(s).

The following chart provides the roles and a mock script to serve as a set of directions. Make a copy for each student and an overhead transparency for you to use as you teach this strategy.

Role	Role Description
Leader	Orally guides the speller through the thinking process
Speller	Uses phonetic, visual, and auditory knowledge to solve the spelling of the word
Researcher(s)	Locates the word in the dictionary, providing support for the leader as he or she helps the speller, and support for the speller after he or she has solved the spelling error

Sample Script

LEADER TO SPELLER: "What is the word you identified as misspelled?"

As the Speller says the word, the Leader puts blank lines for each letter of the word on the board or overhead. For example, the Speller identifies the word, *baby.*

The leader marks _____ _____ _____ _____ on the board or overhead.

LEADER TO RESEARCHER: "Please find the word in the dictionary and check to see if I've used the correct number of spaces. As I help the Speller think this through, please check my spelling, too."

(If the Leader knows the correct spelling, he or she can say, "I know this one, so would you please look it up and wait until the speller finishes.")

LEADER TO SPELLER: "What do you already know about this word? What's the first letter (or initial blend, if applicable)?"

The Leader slowly and clearly articulates the sounds of the word: "Baaaabeee." As the Speller identifies letters, the Leader writes the information down. <u>b a b _</u>

If the Speller gives the Leader the incorrect information, the Leader does not write the incorrect letter in the space. Instead, he or she continues to sound the word out in an effort to get the Speller to self-correct.

If the Speller gives an incorrect letter and does not self-correct, the Leader leaves the space blank. For instance, if the Speller says, " "*b a b e,*" the Leader writes, <u>b a b _</u>.

LEADER TO SPELLER: "You have everything correct but one letter. You should start to trust yourself. The Researcher and I are going to give you a clue. This word ends just like the words *lady, funny,* and *sorry*. Can you think of the correct spelling of any of those words?"

If the Speller responds: "b _a_ b _y_," the Leader offers encouragement like, "Good thinking!" and then writes _b_ _a_ _b_ _y_ on the board. If the Speller doesn't know anything about the *y* ending, then the Leader and the Researcher should share this information with the Speller. If they have any doubt, they should ask the teacher for the information.

LEADER: "Now, please spell the whole word." As the Speller spells, the Leader moves the chalk under each letter. Can you identify where you had your difficulty?"

SPELLER: "I didn't know the word ended in a *y*."

LEADER: "What did you find out that will help you remember this word the next time you use it?"

SPELLER: "Well, some words end in *y*, but have an *e* sound such as *funny* and *baby*."

LEADER: "How are you going to remember it the next time you need to use it?"

SPELLER: "At the end of a word when you hear an *e* sound it may be a *y. Baby, funny, lady, sorry*. I will try to memorize those words."

(The Leader now tries to encourage the Speller to identify any unique way to remember a word. Rhymes, word families, phonetic rules, or a strange mnemonic such as *was* is *saw* backwards or *was* is *as* with a *w*. The rule of thumb is—whatever works for the Speller!)

LEADER: "Okay, let's practice your way for remembering."

LEADER (AFTER PRACTICE): "That's really smart. You should trust yourself."

(Although it may be difficult for some students to do so, the Leader should be encouraged to look the Speller in the eye when saying this.)

LEADER: "The Researcher(s) have located the word in the dictionary for you. Please study the word from the dictionary. Cross out the misspelled word in your draft, and write the correct spelling in the space above the misspelled word."

(Leader repeats process with another word or another Speller.)

Teacher Note: To reinforce this strategy, it is helpful to demonstrate the process for students again, and then ask for someone to assume your role as Leader. Get two Researchers to sit near the new Leader as you coach from the sidelines.

You'll probably need to repeat this process several times over a couple of days. Students should be given a chance to assume each role. Modeling and debriefing also help students learn the strategy. After a group of three or four students models the process for the class, you can debrief by asking: "What did you find out about each role? What did you learn that will improve your skills?"

Once the spelling study groups learn to work independently, it's a good idea to provide 8–12 minutes each day for groups to meet. After group work, the whole class briefly discusses the spelling information they are learning. Rules are entered into the class-made grammar/spelling book. The spelling study groups can also work on lists of basic sight words and the most commonly misspelled words. You can then add these words to the week's spelling list and alert students that you will look for these words in particular to be spelled correctly in edited papers. This process helps students retain the words.

Becoming More Independent

Second Revision and the Confidence Factor

PREPARING FOR THE LESSON

☀ Have available your transparency of the "Phases of the Writing Process" diagram (see page 91), as well as your transparency of the Lesson 11 Study Sheet, "Writing Coach's Prompt," (see page 58).

☀ Give each student a copy of the Lesson 13 Study Sheet, "Second Revision: A Writer/Coach Discussion" (page 71). Make a transparency for your own use.

☀ Gather colored marking pens or pencils for the Second Revision; all students should use the same color, but it should be different from those used in previous marking and editing.

☀ Read and review the following background material: the subsection of "Second Revision," pages 102–105.

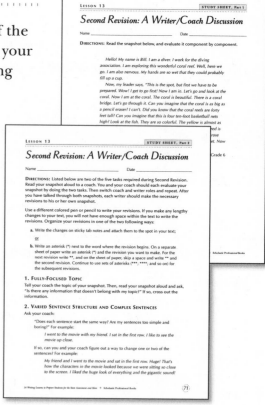

PRESENTING THE LESSON

Second Revision

1. Distribute to each student a copy of the Lesson 13 Study Sheet Parts 1 and 2, "Second Revision: A Writer/Coach Discussion." Place your transparency of the Lesson 13 Study Sheet Part 1 on the overhead.

Pair up your students and tell them that this will be another chance to practice thinking like a writing coach. Have them silently read the snapshot, then instruct them to evaluate the quality of the snapshot and discuss it with their partner, component by component.

Hello! My name is Bill. I am a diver. I work for the diving association. I am exploring this wonderful coral reef. Well, here we go. I am also nervous. My hands are so wet that they could probably fill up a cup.

Now, my leader says, "This is the spot, but first we have to be prepared. Wow!

66

I get to go first! Now I am in. Let's go and look at the coral. Now I am at the coral. The coral is beautiful. There is a coral bridge. Let's go through it. Can you imagine that the coral is as big as a pencil eraser? I can't. Did you know that the coral reefs are forty feet tall? Can you imagine that this is four ten-foot basketball nets high? Look at the fish. They are so colorful. The yellow is almost as bright as the sun. The orange is as bright as a basketball. The red is bright as a rose, and the sea urchin's spikes are as pointy as a rose, also. Wow! Look at that octopus. It shot out as quick as a bullet. Now it is time to go. Nice talking to you again.

—Bill (Grade 6)

2 Invite students to share their reactions to the snapshot. Start by eliciting comments about what works well and what students like about the snapshot. (Responses may include the many specific details and descriptive words, the use of similes, the feeling of excitement the writer creates.) Help students realize that there is also room for improvement. Ask them to make recommendations to the writer for improving his work. Possible suggestions include:

The topic is slightly out of focus. For example, *Hello! My name is Bill.*

Well, here we go. Nice talking to you again. These sentences don't have much to do with the topic.

The time frame is not adequately narrowed. Is it the day he went diving? It seems like he's describing the first three minutes of the dive, but that isn't clear.

The beginning needs to be more dynamic and the ending should tie things up better.

The writer hasn't told the reader when the snapshot occurred.

Even though Bill used some exceptional similes, his sentence structure is repetitive, so the impact of the language is not as great as it could be.

3 Place your transparency, "Phases of the Writing Process," on the overhead and highlight the final box, "Formal Publication." Explain that when a writer prepares a snapshot for formal publication, his or her name goes on the snapshot, and it is printed for others— friends and strangers—to read. In almost all cases, the writer will not be there when the reader reads the snapshot. In short, when a piece of writing is formally published, readers will judge the text without any way for the writer to defend or explain the writing.

Invite students to predict how they might feel, knowing that their names will be on their snapshots and that friends and strangers will read and judge their writing. (Most students admit that this thought is a bit intimidating.) Remind them that the snapshot needs to be so clear that it speaks for itself. They will not be present to explain what they meant to say.

4 Discuss with students the fact that Bill's snapshot has a good deal of potential to become a well-crafted text. If Bill had engaged in a second revision, his readers would have had more compliments and found less to criticize. And Bill's message would have been clearer. Use your transparency of the "Phases of the Writing Process" diagram to highlight "Second Revision." Explain that this phase is an opportunity for students to polish the content of the snapshot before it leaves their hands and goes "public." You might add something like, "As a writer, you assume the responsibility for Second Revision because it gives you a chance to make the kinds of changes that will give you the confidence to let others read your text."

5 Inform students that now is their chance to take their second snapshot through a Second Revision. Ask each pair of students to decide who will be the first writer. Place your transparency of the Lesson 13 Study Sheet, Part 2, on the overhead and explain that each pair is going to use tasks 1 and 5 (located on the bottom portion of the sheet) as a guide for revising. The writer will read his or her snapshot to the writing coach, and then both coach and writer will *talk through* the tasks.

Ask students to look at the Lesson 13 Study Sheet as you read the directions for Part 2 aloud:

Directions: *Listed below are two of the five tasks required during Second Revision. Read your snapshot aloud to a coach. You and your coach should each evaluate your snapshot by doing the two tasks. Then switch coach and writer roles and repeat. After you have talked through both snapshots, each writer should make the necessary revisions to his or her own snapshot.*

Explain that there are actually five tasks for the second revision phase, but for now students will be thinking about only two. Each writer will have five minutes or more to discuss the two tasks. Remind students that both partners are to talk before any partner writes revisions.

6 After pairs have *talked through* both tasks, have them read the remaining directions and allow writers time to make the necessary revisions.

Use a different colored pen or pencil to write your revisions. If you make any lengthy changes to your text, you will not have enough space within the text to write the revisions. Organize your revisions in one of the two following ways:

a. Write the changes on sticky tab notes and attach them to the spot in your text;

or

b. Write an asterisk (*) next to the word where the revision begins. On a separate sheet of paper write an asterisk (*) and the revision you want to make. For the next revision write **, and on the sheet of paper, skip a space and write ** and the second revision. Continue to use sets of asterisks (***; ****; and so on) for the subsequent revisions.

7 After students have completed both parts of the Lesson 13 Study Sheet, ask them to debrief. Here are two possibilities for helping them to debrief:

☀ Say to the writer: *Share a revision that you added to make your sentences more interesting.*

☀ Say to the writing coach: *What did you learn from going through the second revision experience that will cause you to change something you say or do when coaching a writer in the planning phase?* (Use your transparency of the "Phases of the Writing Process" diagram and draw an arrow from "Second Revision" to "Planning.")

8 As an introduction to Second Revision, the tasks included in Lesson 13—Tasks 1 and 5—are enough for one lesson. However, for your reference, do check "Section 3: The Writing Process" for the complete list of second revisions (pages 102–105). It is clear that the full set of tasks is too much to teach in one lesson. For example, "Task 4: Logical/Sequential Order with Smooth Transitions," has only some application to a short assignment, such as a snapshot, but more application to a longer text. So, it is best to teach Task 4 in another lesson. In this way, you can make use of the Study Sheet Extension on pages 104–105 as fits your own students' needs, skill development, and writing experience.

Second Revision: A Writer/Coach Discussion

Name _____   Date _____

DIRECTIONS: Read the snapshot below, and evaluate it component by component.

Hello! My name is Bill. I am a diver. I work for the diving association. I am exploring this wonderful coral reef. Well, here we go. I am also nervous. My hands are so wet that they could probably fill up a cup.

Now, my leader says, "This is the spot, but first we have to be prepared. Wow! I get to go first! Now I am in. Let's go and look at the coral. Now I am at the coral. The coral is beautiful. There is a coral bridge. Let's go through it. Can you imagine that the coral is as big as a pencil eraser? I can't. Did you know that the coral reefs are forty feet tall? Can you imagine that this is four ten-foot basketball nets high? Look at the fish. They are so colorful. The yellow is almost as bright as the sun. The orange is as bright as a basketball. The red is bright as a rose, and the sea urchin's spikes are as pointy as a rose also. Wow! Look at that octopus. It shot out as quick as a bullet. Now it is time to go. Nice talking to you again.

—Bill (Grade 6)

Second Revision: A Writer/Coach Discussion

Name _____ Date _____

DIRECTIONS: Listed below are two of the five tasks required during Second Revision. Read your snapshot aloud to a coach. You and your coach should each evaluate your snapshot by doing the two tasks. Then switch coach and writer roles and repeat. After you have talked through both snapshots, each writer should make the necessary revisions to his or her own snapshot.

Use a different colored pen or pencil to write your revisions. If you make any lengthy changes to your text, you will not have enough space within the text to write the revisions. Organize your revisions in one of the two following ways:

a. Write the changes on sticky tab notes and attach them to the spot in your text;

<u>or</u>

b. Write an asterisk (*) next to the word where the revision begins. On a separate sheet of paper write an asterisk (*) and the revision you want to make. For the next revision write **, and on the sheet of paper, skip a space and write ** and the second revision. Continue to use sets of asterisks (***; ****; and so on) for the subsequent revisions.

1. Fully-Focused Topic

Tell your coach the topic of your snapshot. Then, read your snapshot aloud and ask, "Is there any information that doesn't belong with my topic?" If so, cross out the information.

5. Varied Sentence Structure and Complex Sentences

☀ Ask your coach:

"Does each sentence start the same way? Are my sentences too simple and boring?" For example:

I went to the movie with my friend. I sat in the first row. I like to see the movie up close.

☀ If so, can you and your coach figure out a way to change one or two of the sentences? For example:

My friend and I went to the movie and sat in the first row. Huge! That's how the characters in the movie looked because we were sitting so close to the screen. I liked the huge look of everything and the gigantic sound!

Writing the Third Snapshot

PREPARING FOR THE LESSON

* ☀ Make a copy of the Lesson 14 Study Sheet, "What Do I Already Know?" on page 75 for each student.

* ☀ If necessary, make a fresh copy of the Lesson 11 Study Sheet, "Writing Coach's Prompt," page 58 for each student.

* ☀ Give each student a copy of the Lesson 13 Study Sheet, Part 2, "Second Revision, A Writer/Coach Discussion," on page 71.

* ☀ Have available your transparency of the "Writing Coach's Evaluation Checklist of Snapshot Skills," (original on page 95).

* ☀ Have available your transparency of the "Phases of the Writing Process" diagram (original on page 91).

* ☀ Make a copy of the "Snapshot Scoring Rubric" (pages 76–77) for each student, and prepare an overhead transparency for yourself.

* ☀ Finally, before starting this lesson, be sure to read and review the background information in Section 3, "The Writing Process."

PRESENTING THE LESSON

1 Let students know that they are now going to write their third snapshot, applying the knowledge they have learned while writing the first and second snapshots. For the third snapshot, each writer's goal is to become more independent as a writer, as a writing coach, and in applying the phases of the writing process.

Offer students the following encouragement: "You should trust yourself because you now have two experiences that have taught you a lot, giving you the confidence to be independent." Give each student a copy of the Lesson 14 Study Sheet, "What Do I Already Know?" (page 75). Read the directions and instruct students to complete the study sheet.

Directions: *You have a tremendous amount of knowledge about the writing process stored inside your head by now. Trust yourself. Quickly brainstorm—let your thoughts flow. Think quickly, and* *then web your first thoughts as you ask yourself, "What do I already know about..."*

2   As a follow-up to the study sheet, engage students in a class discussion. On the chalkboard or overhead write: "Classroom Confidence List." Call for volunteers to share what they listed on their study sheets and write each "major snapshot confidence" under your heading. If students have questions, take time for any clarification or elaboration that may be necessary.

3   Let students know that for this third snapshot, you will be gathering data and evaluating their work. Remind them that although you did not collect data during their learning experiences with the first two snapshots, now that they are writing their third snapshot, evaluation is important and can provide them with helpful feedback. Distribute a copy of the "Snapshot Scoring Rubric" to each student and discuss the points system and the criteria for evaluation. Explain that you will collect data from the draft copy, the final copy, and from your observations during the phases. Also, let students know that you will begin to evaluate their coaching skills. Explain that the goal is for them to self-coach, but for now you will evaluate them in pairs. Place your transparency of the "Writing Coach's Evaluation Checklist of Snapshot Skills" on the overhead as you make this point.

It's helpful to realize that there are two critical aspects to enabling students to make the transition from paired to self-coaching—first, consistent use of debriefing and evaluation conferences; and second, the provision of enough time for students to internalize the process. (This is true whether students are learning to write snapshots or longer texts, such as memoirs, or working in new genres, such as essay or mystery writing.) It takes considerable time and practice for students to genuinely absorb the criteria and to learn to become effective listeners and advice givers. For this reason, some teachers make the transition by having students plan in pairs for three or four snapshots, and only then move into self-coaching.

4   Next, point out the conference grid at the bottom of the second page of the rubric. Inform your students that after three drafts, you will meet with each of them individually to talk about the strengths of the drafts and to make recommendations for improvement. If students have questions about anything relating to the evaluation or the rubric, clarify these before continuing. Let them know that this same "Snapshot Scoring Rubric" will be used in all subsequent assignments.

5   Place your transparency of "Phases of the Writing Process" on the overhead. Remind students to trust their knowledge and apply what they know. As you give the directions phase-by-phase, highlight each phase on your transparency. For your reference, the chart on page 74 sums up lesson guidelines and reminders. Notice that ranges are given for many of the time frames. Some flexibility must be built in because the precise time you select for each phase and for your own students will depend on your specific classroom situation and your students' experience. Note, too, that this lesson may take one class period or two.

Phase	Time Frame	Teacher's Reminder
Selecting a Topic	2–3 min.	☀ Someone or something you saw recently... ☀ Narrow the time frame.
Planning	5–7 min. per writer 1 min.	☀ Arrange students in pairs and give each student a copy of the Lesson 11 Study Sheet, "Writing Coach's Prompt." ☀ Using the "Writing Coach's Evaluation Checklist of Snapshot Skills," practice evaluating a few students. After planning, share your findings.
Drafting	20–25 min.	☀ Once directions are given, circulate among students and observe their writing behaviors. After the drafting period is complete, report to the whole class about what you noted during their work.
First Revision	2–3 min.	☀ This is a brief task with a single focus. Some teachers expect 100 percent accountability.
Informal Publication	4 min.	☀ Inform students that time limits allow four one-minute presentations. Students who volunteer will need to practice before presenting. Explain that writers often practice aloud, with a pencil in hand. ☀ Elicit feed back from listeners.
Second Revision*	3–4 min. per writer 5–10 min. 2 min.	☀ Give each student a copy of the Lesson 13 Study Sheet, "Second Revision, A Writer/Coach Discussion," and assign new partners. Observe sessions and report your findings. ☀ Give writers time to make second revisions. ☀ Debrief by asking writers to share some second revisions. Encourage listeners to applaud a writer's changes.
Editing	1–2 min. per task	☀ One task at a time, have students reread their snapshots to edit for capitalization, identifying misspelled words, and solving misspellings. (The remaining portion of the spelling strategy, "From Problem Solving to Trusting Yourself," can be continued during spelling instruction.)
Informal Publication	4 min.	☀ Tell students that time limits allow four one-minute presentations. Students who volunteer will need to practice.

* If you split the lesson into two parts, this is the recommended dividing point.

What Do I Already Know?

Name _____   Date _____

DIRECTIONS: You have a tremendous amount of knowledge about the writing process stored inside your head by now. Briefly brainstorm—let your thoughts flow. Think quickly, and then web your first thoughts as you ask yourself, "What do I already know about..."

(my strengths as a snapshot writer)

(my strengths as a snapshot coach)

(the phases of the writing process)

List any questions you'd like to ask:

1. _____

2. _____

3. _____

My major snapshot confidence is

_____

_____

Name _____   Date _____

6 = Application of skill is excellent
3 = Application of skill is just adequate and could be improved
1 = Application of skill is still inadequate and needs work

Writing Process Phase and Standard	Date	Date	Date	Date	Date
Selecting a Topic					
☀ selects scenario and narrows time frame					
Planning					
☀ plans effectively with a coach					
☀ plans effectively by self-coaching					
Drafting					
☀ uses full time for writing					
☀ drafts fluently and mulls ideas					
☀ takes risks with exceptional language					
☀ does all tasks independently					
First Revision					
☀ has no missing words					
Second Revision					
☀ stays focused on topic					
☀ has clearly expressed content					
☀ selects exceptional word choice					
☀ has logical, sequential order with smooth transitions					
☀ uses varied sentence structure and complex sentences					
☀ does all tasks independently					

16 Writing Lessons to Prepare Students for the State Assessment and More ☀ Scholastic Professional Books

Writing Process Phase and Standard	Date	Date	Date	Date	Date
Editing					
☀ applies capitalization (proper nouns and the personal pronoun *I*, beginning of sentence)					
☀ applies end-of-sentence punctuation					
☀ identifies misspelled words					
☀ corrects misspellings					
☀ performs all tasks independently					
Informal Publication					
☀ delivers an oral presentation clearly and directly					
☀ listens attentively and provides writer feedback					
☀ knows how to construct book parts: cover, table of contents, dedication					
☀ has legible, well-formed handwriting; applies computer word processing					
TOTAL SCORE					

Student/Teacher Conference

Content of Discussion	Notes with Student's Initials
Recommendations for improvement of next two drafts: ☀ student's recommendation for improvement ☀ teacher's recommendation for improvement	
Analyze the major strengths of three drafts: ☀ student's comments about standards and process ☀ teacher's comments about standards and process	

Editing for Capitalization and Punctuation

PREPARING FOR THE LESSON

☀ Read and review the background material, "Editing" (pages 106 to 108) of Section 3. Because this material features a series of teaching steps and tips that relate directly to this lesson, you may wish to make a photocopy of the subsection and keep it handy.

☀ Review and have available for yourself a copy of "Capitalization Strategy # 3: Applying Capitalization Knowledge"(page 82) and "Punctuation Strategies #1 through #4" (pages 82–83), all Lesson 15 Teaching Strategies.

☀ Give each student a copy of the Lesson 15 "Snapshot Model," on page 81, and make an overhead transparency for your own use. Alternately, if you have been using your own snapshot script throughout, use the model as a guide to create your own version without punctuation and capitalization, then make a copy of that version for each student and a transparency for yourself.

☀ Assemble different colored marking pens or pencils for your students; they should use one color for the capitalization strategy and one for the punctuation strategies.

PRESENTING THE LESSON

1 Explain to students that in this lesson, they will be focusing on an overall capitalization strategy that picks up from the editing techniques they learned earlier in Lesson 12, and that they will also be learning and applying several punctuation strategies. As they did in Lesson 12, students will use one strategy at a time, since it is much easier to learn the strategies this way. Eventually, with more practice, the strategies will become automatic, and students should be able to apply several at one time.

2 Place the snapshot model on the overhead and distribute a copy to each student. Invite students to read through the snapshot and share their initial reactions, for instance: How well can they make sense of it? Can they read it fluently as it is currently written? Elicit recommendations for corrections that might clarify the meaning and the fluency of the snapshot.

3 Tell students that they will be using "Punctuation Strategy #1: And for the Love of the Run-On Sentence" for their initial work on the snapshot model. Distribute a colored pen or pencil to each student. Follow the directions for Punctuation Strategy # 1.

4 Explain to students that they will be using this model to edit for several different kinds of capitalization, including both those that were the focus of Lesson 12 (proper nouns and the pronoun *I*), and two other common instances (beginnings of sentences and important words in titles). Remind students to use a different colored pen or pencil from that used for the punctuation strategy. Follow the directions for "Capitalization Strategy #3: Applying Capitalization Knowledge."

5 Ask students to tell you what is still missing from the snapshot model. (It should now have corrected capitalization and no run-on sentences, but still lack end-of-sentence punctuation marks.) After students have identified the missing punctuation element, instruct them to follow the directions for "Punctuation Strategy #2: Put Back in the End-of-Sentence Marks."

6 Next, have students read and apply the remaining two punctuation strategies to the snapshot model. Strategy # 3 focuses on the use of quotation marks, and Strategy #4 is essentially an overall check for comma usage.

7 *(Note: You may wish to engage in the following steps of this lesson in a separate time block.)* If students have access to computers, ask them to type the final copy of their third snapshot. If students do not have computers readily available, you can use this exercise as a handwriting assignment as well as an editing task. In either case, instruct students to format their text in a way that is similar to the snapshot model, using a large font (or good-sized hand script) and providing ample space between the lines. They should:

☀ remove all beginning-of-sentence capital letters except for the first one

☀ remove all end-of-sentence punctuation except for the last one and replace the deleted punctuation marks with the word *and*

☀ remove all intra-sentence punctuation including commas, quotation marks, colons, or semicolons

☀ save their work on a disk and print two copies, or make two photocopies of their handwritten original

☀ write their names on their snapshot

8 Inform students that they will take on roles of "writer" and "editor." Ask each student to label one snapshot copy as "Master Copy." On this master copy, each student, as "writer," should then strike out the unnecessary *ands* and place a slash where he or she thinks the end-of-sentence punctuation mark should be.

9 Arrange students in pairs. Ask each pair to exchange the unmarked snapshot copy and follow the same marking procedure to edit his or her partner's snapshot. The editor should put his or her name on the writer's snapshot (for example: "Editor: Alice Jones") directly below the writer's name and then return the edited copy to the writer.

10 Finally, ask the writer in each pair to read the editor's markings and compare them to the master copy. If there is not a consensus, the partners should discuss their logic with one another, and eventually reach agreement. It will be helpful for you to circulate among the pairs to resolve any differences in opinion.

11 Follow up the completed lesson by debriefing with the entire class. Ask students to describe the specific function for each grammar rule and to summarize the different editing strategies they have learned.

Snapshot Model

(for use with Capitalization Strategy 3 and Punctuation Strategies 1–4)

getting his own breakfast

This morning my husband tall and handsome
stood in front of the stove cooking his eggs
and as usual he was dressed for work
looking as neat as a groom on his wedding
day and he yawned and stretched and
whined in a self-pitying voice gosh i wish
someone would cook my breakfast for me
and then he looked at me smiled and said
and but i know how busy you already are
and you don't need one more thing to do and
i blushed on the outside but on the inside i
felt like an accomplished woman

PUNCTUATION STRATEGY #1:

And for the Love of the Run-On Sentence

☀ Pair students. Ask each pair to work together to identify unnecessary *ands* in the snapshot model, page 81. Have them use their red pencils or pens to strike out each unnecessary *and*. Next, ask them to use another color to make a clearly visible slash mark where the end-of-sentence punctuation should be. Allow 2–3 minutes for pairs to work. Bring the whole class together and, using your overhead copy, ask students to discuss their findings and reach a consensus. Mark the final decisions on your copy.

☀ Ask the class to discuss what they have discovered. Help elicit the notion that as a writer figures out where to start and stop sentences, he or she is really asking, "How can I make my point clear for a reader? Should I put one idea in this sentence? Two ideas? How many ideas are too many for this sentence?" Only when the writer has decided these things, will it be clear which sentences legitimately require the connecting word "and" and which sentences should stop with one idea.

CAPITALIZATION STRATEGY # 3:

Applying Capitalization Knowledge

☀ Ask each writer to edit the snapshot model (page 81) to make capital letter corrections for:

- proper nouns
- beginnings of sentences
- the pronoun I
- important words in titles

☀ Have students work in pairs to determine a logical explanation for their use of each capital letter. They should be able to answer this question for each: "Which of the four categories does this use fit into?" If students have questions, encourage them to refer to their grammar texts and other available grammar books and resources to locate the rule for each capital letter correction.

☀ If your students are publishing a class-made grammar book, as suggested in Capitalization Strategy # 1 (page 61), ask them to enter the rules into the book.

PUNCTUATION STRATEGY # 2:

Put Back in the End-of-Sentence Marks

☀ Once the capital letters are restored to the snapshot model (page 81), ask students to work in pairs to insert the end-of-sentence marks: periods, exclamation marks, or question marks.

☀ Advise students that you want partners to reach agreement on the appropriate mark and to be able to state their reason for selecting that mark.

☀ Conduct a whole-class discussion, asking students to make a rule that will help them decide how to separate or combine sentences. Place the rule in the class-made grammar book.

PUNCTUATION STRATEGY # 3:

Quotation Expertise

☀ Have students read through the snapshot model (page 81) to identify any instances of one character speaking directly to another. (There are two such instances.) Once students have identified the correct spots, ask them where and how quotation marks should be used. If students need help, refer them to their grammar books and other resources.

☀ Next, insert quotation marks in the proper places on your overhead transparency and have students do the same on their own copies of the snapshot model.

☀ Conduct a whole-class discussion, asking students to put into their own words the rule for using quotation marks with direct speech. If students are compiling a class-made grammar book, add this rule to the book.

PUNCTUATION STRATEGY # 4:

Any Left-Over Commas?

☀ Ask students to read through the snapshot model on page 81 again—this time to identify if the snapshot needs additional commas. (There are several instances.) Once students have identified the correct spots, ask them where and how commas should be used. If students need help, refer them to their grammar books and other resources to review comma rules and learn those that have not already been covered.

☀ Then, insert the commas in the proper places on your overhead transparency and have students do the same on their own copies of the snapshot model.

☀ Conduct a whole-class discussion, inviting students to formulate rules for these comma applications. If they are compiling a class-made grammar book, place these rules in the book.

Formal Publication and Evaluation

PREPARING FOR THE LESSON

☀ Read and review the background material, "Formal Publication and Evaluation" (pages 109 to 110) in Section 3. Because this material features a series of teaching steps and tips that relate directly to this lesson, you may wish to photocopy the pages and keep them handy.

☀ Prepare a personalized copy of the model letter on page 86. Have this and the "Snapshot Readers' Comments" sheet on page 87 available.

☀ The "Phases of the Writing Process" transparency (original on page 91) should also be available.

☀ Students will need the Lesson 3 Study Sheet, "Get Ready! Get Set! How Does That Feel?" which should be stored in each writer's folder.

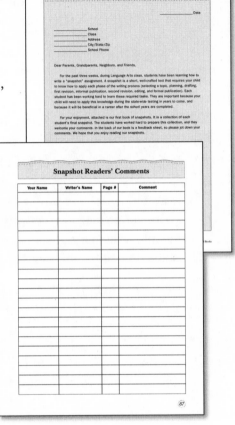

PRESENTING THE LESSON

1 Place your "Phases of the Writing Process" transparency on the overhead. Highlight the final phase, Formal Publication, and invite students to get ready for this phase by asking, "So, are you ready to prepare your third snapshot for formal publication?"

2 If a computer lab or sufficient classroom computers are available, the whole class will be able to work simultaneously on their drafts of the third snapshot. If you have access to only one or a few computers, you will have to work out a rotation system for typing. Give students a uniform format for right and left margins. (When snapshots are placed in the final classroom book, margins must be consistent.)

3 Remind students to provide a title for their snapshots and to type a byline—their first and last names—under the title or at the bottom of the text.

4 Tell students that you will be circulating around the room, acting as an "outside editor," while they are typing their drafts. An outside editor makes final corrections to a writer's text. As you circulate among students, make recommendations for capital letters, punctuation, and spelling. Carry sticky tab notes or pieces of scrap paper with you, and when you notice a spelling error, encourage the writer to correct the error using the "Think-It-Through—From Problem Solving to Trusting Yourself" strategy learned in Lesson 12.

5 When students are finished typing, they should each save and print a hard copy of their text.

6 Hold a whole-class discussion to elicit suggestions for a title for the collection. Write student ideas on the chalkboard or overhead and have the class vote to select one. Then ask students for suggestions for a dedication, and follow the same voting procedure to choose one.

7 Ask for two student volunteers to prepare the cover. Explain to these students that they'll need to type the title, designate the author (Mr., Mrs., or Ms. _____'s class), and illustrate the cover, based on the title that has been selected.

8 Call on two other volunteers to number the pages in the lower right hand corner and collate the stack.

9 Insert your letter to parents and others as the top page and the feedback sheet as the last page.

10 Ask for three volunteers to prepare the table of contents using a computer. The title of each snapshot, the writer's name, and the page number should be listed.

11 Ask each student to look through his or her writer's folder and find the Lesson 3 Study Sheet, "Get Ready! Get Set! How Does That Feel?" Ask students to respond to the same question they answered three weeks ago, this time using a different color pen or pencil. Invite them to talk about the difference in their responses, then and now. Each student should put his or her name on the paper and write in today's date. Then, have students turn the paper over and make a web or jot down a list of everything they now know about the writing process.

12 As a final step, celebrate authorship. Here are a few suggestions of what some teachers do:

☀ Students read aloud their formally published snapshots. (A writer can read his or her own work or invite a fellow student to read the snapshot.)

☀ Listeners sketch the writer's snapshot and give the sketches to the writer. (Have 4" x 6" cards or sheets of paper prepared ahead of time for this.)

☀ Students decorate the cover of their writer's folder.

☀ An audience (parents, friends, or other classes) is invited and students read aloud their formally published snapshots.

_____ Date

_____ School
_____ Class
_____ Address
_____ City/State/Zip
_____ School Phone

Dear Parents, Grandparents, Neighbors, and Friends,

For the past three weeks, during Language Arts class, students have been learning how to write a "snapshot" assignment. A snapshot is a short, well-crafted text that requires your child to know how to apply each phase of the writing process (selecting a topic, planning, drafting, first revision, informal publication, second revision, editing, and formal publication). Each student has been working hard to learn these required tasks. They are important because your child will need to apply this knowledge during the state-wide testing in years to come, and because it will be beneficial in a career after the school years are completed.

For your enjoyment, attached is our first book of snapshots. It is a collection of each student's final snapshot. The students have worked hard to prepare this collection, and they welcome your comments. In the back of our book is a feedback sheet, so please jot down your comments. We hope that you enjoy reading our snapshots.

Writing and publishing snapshots, snapshot extensions, and longer texts are ongoing instructional events in our classroom. You are invited to visit our classroom so you can learn more about our writing program. If you wish to visit, please contact me.

Sincerely,

_____

Snapshot Readers' Comments

Your Name	Writer's Name	Page #	Comment

The Writing Process: Phase-by-Phase Background Information

THIS SECTION PROVIDES BACKGROUND INFORMATION FOR EACH PHASE OF THE writing process. You might think of it as a kind of compendium of supplementary material for your reference and information as you teach the lessons. For each phase, the discussion is organized as follows:

MAJOR GOALS AND TASKS

☀ major goals and tasks the snapshot writer must think about and attend to during this phase

BACKGROUND INFORMATION AND TEACHING TIPS

☀ descriptions that provide background information about the phase

☀ tips that offer specific suggestions to help you teach the phase

The diagram on page 91, "Phases of the Writing Process," summarizes each phase of the writing process and graphically presents the relationships among the phases. This diagram represents an essential element of many of the lessons in Section 2. You should consider making a transparency of the diagram so that it will be available to you as an instructional tool. As your students gain more experience applying each phase of the process, it will be helpful for each of them to have his or her own photocopy of the diagram, too. Students can keep the diagram in their snapshot writer's folder as a checklist for their learning and as a handy reference.

Selecting a Topic

Major Goals and Tasks

When selecting a topic, the writer chooses the content of the text and narrows the topic in terms of its time.

The writer might describe this phase in these words:

> "I am going to think of a topic—the main character and what's going on, a small scenario in time—and how much time the scenario represents."

Background Information and Teaching Tips

1. When students know that they are working toward a snapshot that will be prepared for final publication, they approach the writing assignment differently than when they are writing for your eyes only. Realizing that their snapshots will be placed in a class collection to be read by others, students write with a different kind of commitment, purpose, and energy. From the beginning, therefore, let students know that they are working toward formal publication of their snapshots. And from the beginning, it will help students if you are specific about your expectations. Explain to students that each writer will learn to:

   ☀ write a well-crafted snapshot that, from the first sentence to the last, creates a dynamic visual image and holds the reader's attention

   ☀ gain control (independence) over each phase of the writing process

2. When confronted with choosing a topic, sometimes students draw a blank. Always give an example of what *you* are planning to write to jump-start students' thinking. Ask students to share their topics to get more ideas flowing.

   For example, when you give the snapshot assignment, ask students to think of someone or something—like a particular person or a pet—that they saw that morning. Have them identify what happened to the person or pet (a short event, a scenario). Finally, ask students to identify the amount of time that the event took to unfold. The following examples make good topics for a snapshot:

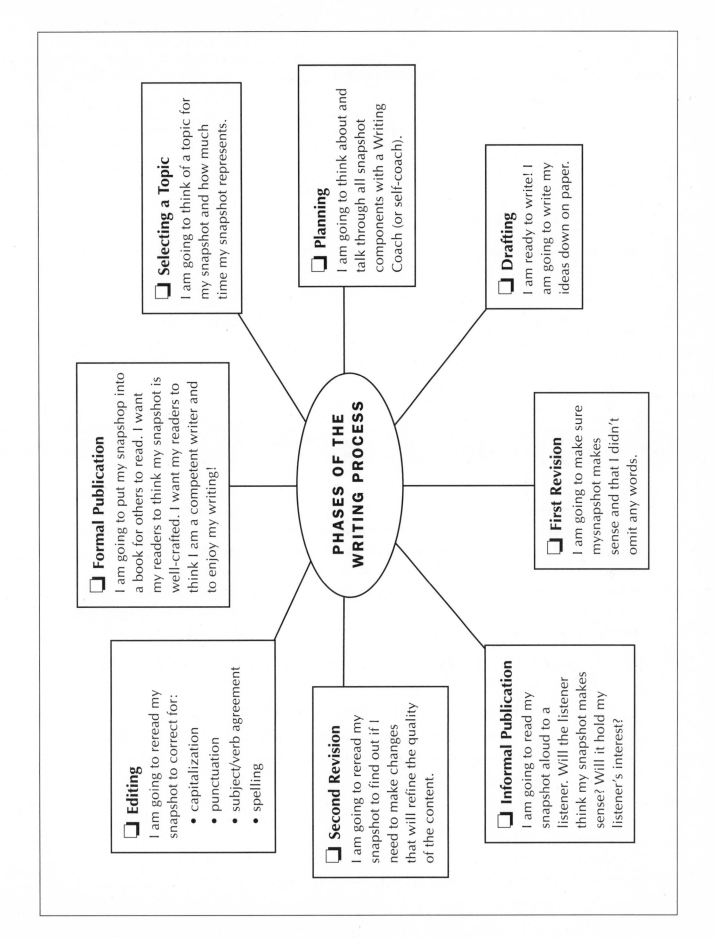

Selecting a Topic
I am going to think of a topic for my snapshot and how much time my snapshot represents.

Planning
I am going to think about and talk through all snapshot components with a Writing Coach (or self-coach).

Drafting
I am ready to write! I am going to write my ideas down on paper.

Formal Publication
I am going to put my snapshop into a book for others to read. I want my readers to think my snapshot is well-crafted. I want my readers to think I am a competent writer and to enjoy my writing!

PHASES OF THE WRITING PROCESS

First Revision
I am going to make sure mysnapshot makes sense and that I didn't omit any words.

Editing
I am going to reread my snapshot to correct for:
• capitalization
• punctuation
• subject/verb agreement
• spelling

Second Revision
I am going to reread my snapshot to find out if I need to make changes that will refine the quality of the content.

Informal Publication
I am going to read my snapshot aloud to a listener. Will the listener think my snapshot makes sense? Will it hold my listener's interest?

Character	What Happened?	Time Span
my husband	fixing his breakfast	1 or 2 minutes
my cat	jumped on my bed to get me up	about 5 minutes
me	My mom waited in the car in the driveway to take me to school, but there was a huge puddle I had to cross.	about 3 minutes
an old man	On the way to school, through the bus window, I saw an old man weaving down the sidewalk.	1 minute
my hamster	As I ate breakfast, I watched my hamster in his cage.	about 5 minutes

Sometimes teachers worry that students will merely latch onto another's idea. However, the snapshot is a very non-threatening writing assignment because the selection of a topic comes from the writer's direct and current experience. Hearing others' ideas can help unlock a student's own experiences. This is especially true if you welcome all original and plausible selections by providing positive and enthusiastic feedback. Often the reluctance to think of an original idea occurs because the student doesn't, at this point, trust his or her judgment; your encouragement can help build that trust. And remember, students experience new sights and events each day, so this exercise can be used as a never-ending topic generator for snapshots.

3. Help students learn how to narrow the topic by identifying the event's passage of time. Students often don't understand that a few moments of a life experience have the potential to become a page or two of text. Frequently, they try to write about something that happened over a long span of time. For example, many students select a topic such as, "My Vacation" or "A Day at the Theme Park." When broad topics like this are selected, a boring passage often results. The text is nothing but a series of run-on events, lacking detail and barren of interesting language.

Here is a tip about how to talk a student's topic down from a broad subject to a specific snapshot:

Student: I'm going to write about my trip to King's Island.

Teacher: You are going to write about your trip to King's Island, the part of your trip when... (Hold your hands wide apart.)

Student: The second day I went to King's Island...

Teacher: From that second day, you are going to write about when... (Hold your hands closer together.)

Student: When I went on the roller coaster ride.

Teacher: The few minutes on the roller coaster that you... (Hold your hands even closer together.)

After you have gone through this process several times with students, they will begin to realize that a few moments in time have the potential to be the topic of a well-crafted text. Students will better acquire this know-how when writing the second snapshot, and by the third one, most writers should demonstrate the ability to select and narrow a topic.

Planning

Major Goals and Tasks

When planning a draft, a writer uses a scheme such as talking through a plan to get ideas flowing and to produce a fluent, natural-sounding text.

The writer might describe this phase in these words:

> "I am going to *think about* and *talk through* all the snapshot components with a Writing Coach (or I may self-coach). I will focus specifically on:
> - who, where, when, and what's going on
> - interesting, exceptional language
> - a dynamic beginning and a tie-up ending."

Background Information and Teaching Tips

1. In one way or another, all state writing rubrics include requirements focused on fluency, language use, and tone. The Indiana writing rubric describes these requirements within the category called *Style and Voice:*

   Style: Writer demonstrates exceptional writing technique.

   Writing is fluent and easy to read.

   Writer uses techniques (i.e. literary conventions such as imagery and dialogue, and/or literary genres such as humor or suspense).

   Voice: Writer effectively adjusts language and tone to task and reader.

   Writer has a unique perspective; it may be original, authoritative, lively, and/or exciting.

   These requirements mean that students are accountable for creating an easy-to-read, natural-sounding text that creates imagery in a reader's mind. The text must address the reader in a tone that is lively, unique, and original.

2. One excellent method of helping students learn how to meet these requirements is the collaborative planning scheme called a "coaching session." Essentially a pairing of students as writer and writing coach, this is the approach followed in this book. This teaming concept provides the writer with a coach to facilitate the development of the writer's orally articulated plan. Articulating a plan gives the writer a means of achieving text fluency and the confidence to write an authoritative, lively text. The writing coach is learning the rubric expectations as he or she coaches the writer, so that when the roles are switched, the coach is already informed about the writing experience. Because it offers students the chance to take both roles, the team experience is also effective training for the eventual goal, self-coaching, a skill that is essential during independent writing assignments.

   Teachers often ask if they should give the students a copy of the rubric. While it *is* a good idea to give them the rubric, this is not the key issue. This listing will remain of little value unless the writer understands how the rubric descriptors relate to the construction of a text. During coaching, a writer talks through his or her plan in relationship to each rubric descriptor, and the coach facilitates the writer's thinking. In this way, the experience teaches the meaning of the rubric descriptors in a dynamic, applied manner.

3. The ultimate outcomes for coaching are that both the writer and the coach learn how to:

   ☀ become a better writer

   ☀ self-coach

4. Take your time when you first begin modeling how to coach. It's important that you train your students very carefully. Remember that you are demonstrating step-by-step procedures and outlining expectations from your state rubric and state standards. Study the "Writing Coach's Evaluation Checklist of Snapshot Skills" (on page 95), and modify it according to your own state's requirements. Make certain that each skill you want your students to learn is highlighted in the coaching modeling sessions you hold with your students. After students have had adequate experience writing snapshots, you can begin to use the checklist as an evaluation instrument.

Student's Name _____

Rating Scale: 6 = excellent application of skill
3 = acceptable application of skill
1 = application of skill not yet adequate

SKILL: The coach listens and probes for snapshot components:	Date	Date	Date	Date	Date	Date	Date	Date	Date	Date
asks who is in the snapshot; asks about physical characteristics: appearance, clothing, age										
asks about *who* in terms of personality: character and what was said or done										
asks about *who* in terms of feelings										
asks about what's going on										
asks about how much time the snapshot represents										
asks about where it takes place										
asks about when it takes place										
probes for more details										
listens for interesting, exceptional language										
listens for a dynamic beginning										
listens for a tie-up ending										
gets writer to talk a lot										
encourages writer to mull over word choices										
listens attentively										
supports with positive, constructive comments										
debriefs with writer and with self										
applies component recommendations to own writing										

Notes:

Drafting

Major Goals and Tasks

When drafting, the writer takes the ideas that were articulated during the planning phase and translates them from thoughts into writing, from head to paper.

The writer might describe this phase in these words:

> "I am ready to write! I am going to write my ideas down on paper. I am going to:
>
> - think and write from my heart and let the words flow
>
> - focus upon ideas first and editing (spelling, punctuation, etc.) later
>
> - mull over in my mind interesting, exceptional language choices
>
> - write a dynamic beginning and a tie-up ending
>
> - attract and hold my reader
>
> - feel secure enough to take risks
>
> - debrief and learn from the writing experience."

Background Information and Teaching Tips

1. Drafting means that the time has come for the writer to put pencil to paper. Traditionally, when this moment arrives, teachers report that masses of students suddenly head for the pencil sharpener, nerves seem to be on edge, and some version of this inevitable question arises, "How many sentences do I have to write?" In contrast, responses during the snapshot assignment are quite different. Because students have already been involved in two phases of the writing process, they have already gained a jump start for their thinking; the articulation during the planning phases has set fluency and confidence into motion. So, drafting might well be called, "Ready! Set! Write!" or "Sustained Silent Write (SSW)" because the students really are ready to write.

2. Help students understand that the most difficult and challenging aspect of writing a text is to get one's ideas on paper in a focused, logical, and interesting manner and that this is true for everyone. Choosing just the right words to make a text appeal to a reader takes a lot of concentration. Encourage students to write from the heart and remind them to trust the knowledge they have gained while selecting a topic and planning.

3. Regardless of your grade level, it's best to begin with a brief amount of time for the drafting phase and gradually increase the time. Initially, an appropriate amount of time is about 10 to 13 minutes. You might take a vote among students, asking them to decide which (9–10 minutes minimum to 13–14 minutes maximum) they wish to write. Eventually 20–30 minutes of SSW is a common time frame. Once students become effective planners, teachers report that students usually need more time. In fact, your students will soon begin to request more SSW time!

4. When you first begin the drafting phase, don't allow anyone to start writing until all students have pencils sharpened, paper ready, topic selected, and the planning completed. It is very disruptive to others when some students get up from their desks to sharpen pencils, or when someone calls out, "I don't know what to write!" Remember that the coaching experience has prepared writers to write. The risk of failure has been minimized because students know they will have the opportunity to revise. So, during SSW, the room is to be quiet because writers need to concentrate. Remind students that the sound of pencil-to-paper should be the only sound anyone in the room hears.

   Note: Once your students become more independent in dealing with the writing process, they will be working on different phases at different times. However, when first learning, it's good advice—for them and for you—to have the whole class working on the same phase.

5. During drafting, writers must make interesting, challenging, lively, dynamic, exceptional, risk-taking word choices. This requirement comes directly from Indiana's writing rubric, but it tends to be the case in every state. When you check the requirements found in your state's rubric, you'll likely find a comparable or similar expectation.

   Because the writer must take risks with words at this point, it's important to encourage students to use the words and phrases that were used during the coaching session. If there is uncertainty about the spelling of a particular word, the student should simply write down the known parts, draw a line under the word, and continue with the text. For example, if the writer wants to use the word *fascination*, but is uncertain about the spelling, he or she should write: <u>*fas shun*</u>. The line indicates that the writer will assume the responsibility for fixing it later, during the editing phase.

   Explain to students that when a writer gets hung up on the spelling of one word, his or her train of thought is likely to be disrupted. Time spent stewing over correct spellings during the drafting stage is likely to diminish the quality of the content. Let students know that they shouldn't compromise the quality of the content for concerns about spelling by saying something like, "Correct spelling is very important, but not during drafting. Focus on what you want to say and how you want to say it. You can fix your spelling errors later, during the editing phase."

6. Train writers to skip lines when preparing a draft so they will have room to include revisions and editing markings. Some teachers instruct students to place an X on the first line directly to the left of the red vertical margin line and then make an X on every other line down to the bottom of the paper. Students write only on the X-marked lines.

7. When writers first begin drafting, it will be very helpful for you to write, too. On the overhead or chalkboard, model the process a writer goes through as he or she is drafting a well-crafted text. (If you use an overhead, turn the light off while writing.) As you write, model how you may sometimes omit words—since ideas always flow faster than the pencil. Model how you take risks with vocabulary and how you underline uncertain spellings. When modeling, stop writing, look puzzled, think, get an idea, then resume writing. As you resume writing, indicate with facial expression that you have confidence in your thinking and are pleased with your ideas.

    When your students begin drafting, it is important to step away from them, out of their space and into your own. When first starting to write, some students become edgy and want to depend upon you. Encourage them to solve their own problems. If someone is a reluctant starter, reassure them with your words: "Trust your coaching experience. Trust yourself and just get started. You can do this!" Your students need to understand that drafting a text is a problem-solving event, and that fluency and confidence flow naturally from a good planning phase.

8. Some students stop writing prior to the designated time. "I'm finished, I'm done!" says the body language and facial expression. From a distance, quietly catch the writer's attention, gently move your hand as if you are writing in the air, indicating to the writer that he or she should keep writing. In most instances this or other mimed signals you devise will communicate your expectations, and the writer will get his or her thoughts going and continue writing. If you try to help the writer by speaking, you will disrupt the thinking process of others, undermining your goal for Sustained Silent Writing. Remember that the coaching session prepared the writer for the drafting phase and that he or she has a good deal of background knowledge to call on. You can also remind students *before* they begin drafting, that if they have finished before the time is up, it is always a good idea to reread what they have written, and act as a self coach, searching for more snapshot details.

    When the selected time (usually not enough for most students) is up, ask all writers to complete the sentence they are currently writing. It's also a good idea to make a comment such as, "Well, you've been writing for ____ minutes. As I look around, I can see that some of you are still writing." This lets early finishers know that many classmates are still writing and that you consider this to be a reasonable and necessary amount of time.

9. Sometimes students will just stop writing, claiming that their ideas are blocked or their thinking is stymied. Explain that at one time or another this happens to all

writers. Then encourage them anew to write from the heart. This advice gives a writer permission to tap into and to trust instincts, emotions, and feelings. It also tells a student that you are confident that he or she has something worthwhile to say and write.

First Revision

Major Goals and Tasks

When engaging in first revision, the writer checks to make certain that the text makes sense and that no words have been omitted.

The writer might describe this phase in these words:

> "I am going to make sure my snapshot makes sense and that I didn't omit any words."

Background Information and Teaching Tips

1. During the drafting of a text, a competent writer has a head full of ideas that flow rapidly—much faster than the pencil, pen, or computer keys. Writers' ideas can flow so quickly that they may inadvertently omit words. Writers may think they wrote the words on the page, but they actually didn't. Tell students this is a common occurrence, and therefore, before moving on to informal or formal publication, a writer is accountable for making certain that the text makes sense. First revision is a means of proofreading to find out if all the words intended to be in the text are actually there.

2. In first revision, each writer carefully rereads his or her text and inserts each missing word with a caret symbol (^). This is a critical phase, and students need to know that they are fully accountable for this task. Let students know that you will be observing them as they engage in first revision. You might say, "If you are doing this correctly, I will see you pointing to each word, and I'll know that you are thinking about your writing and giving your snapshot full, complete attention." Remind students to use these two questions as they check their snapshots during first revision:

   ☀ Does each sentence make sense?

   ☀ Did I leave out any words?

3. Often students are unaccustomed to proofreading their writing. After they've written a draft, you may see students shove the paper to the corner of the desk with

that same body language that says, "I'm finished! I'm done!" This happens when writers don't understand that they are engaged in an ongoing process of rethinking and revision and when they don't realize the value of taking time to reread. The teacher's job, at this point, is to help the student replace the sting of mistake with the celebration of revision. A writer's use of the caret is evidence that he or she is bringing spit and polish to the text. The key is that an omitted word is not a "mistake," but is evidence that the writer has had a multitude of intelligent thoughts.

So, celebrate the caret! Really play it up. As writers engage in first revision and you watch over a student's shoulder, you can say things like, "Wow! You're terrific at engaging in first revision. Your pencil is finally doing what your brain wanted in the first place. That's what a real writer does! _____ (name the student's favorite author) would be proud of you, and you should feel proud of yourself because you're taking control of first revision." This seemingly small instructional scene gives the writer an opportunity to feel the power that comes from making effective change.

4. Another way to help students become accountable for first revision is to create an audience for the writer. As we've seen, when writers know their text will gain public attention, they become more committed to the revision task. After you've provided adequate time for engaging in first revision of the snapshot, you can choose student volunteers who have successfully inserted missing words into their texts to read aloud to an audience of classmates. They can read the portion of the text that had an omitted word, saying "At first I had _____ (reads the un-revised sentence), and now I have _____ (reads the revised sentence). "

5. Remind your students that they are accountable for first revision. As writers become skilled and as first revision becomes a habit, you can establish a checklist that holds each writer 100 percent accountable. The privilege of reading aloud a snapshot or giving it to another reader can be reserved for those students who have achieved this goal. Some teachers place first revision into the writing portion of a grade book and evaluate the skill using Pass/Fail criteria. Others maintain checklist data in a binder or on a computer data form. Of course, you should use the format that works best for you. One possible format follows.

First Revision

Name	10-10-02/ Text	10-25-02/ Text	10-30-02/ Text	11-12-02/ Text	11-20-02/ Text
Alice A.	100%/snapshot	100%/snapshot	100%/lit log	100%/lit log	100% /journal
Jack B.	100% /snapshot	0%/snapshot	100%/lit log	100%/lit log	100% /journal
Sam D.	0%/snapshot	0%/snapshot	100%/lit log	100%/lit log	100% /journal

Informal Publication

Major Goals and Tasks

When engaging in informal publication, the writer shares a draft by reading it aloud to a listener or small group of listeners.

The writer might describe this phase in these words:

> "I am going to read my snapshot aloud to a listener. Will the listener think my snapshot makes sense? Will it hold my listener's interest?"

Background Information and Teaching Tips

1. Motivation to write well and commitment to do the best job possible increase substantially when writers know they will be sharing their work with an audience. Informal publication provides a ready-made audience of peers. Your job during this phase is to find as many opportunities as possible for in-class and out-of-class audiences.

2. After students have finished drafting, you can present this option to them, suggesting perhaps, "There are four one-minute openings for informal publication. Which four writers want to take advantage of this opportunity?" This is also the time to explain that there are some expectations that must be met when writers share their texts aloud. The reading should be:

   ☀ loud enough for everyone to hear

   ☀ delivered fluently, that is, with expression, intonation, and inflection

3. Give all students one minute to practice reading aloud before you select the four presenters. Be forewarned—it will get noisy! Before you choose the students who will read aloud, tell the class that there will be subsequent opportunities for other students to present their work and remind them that at the end of the process, everyone will have a chance to formally publish his or her snapshot.

4. After each presentation, encourage listeners to respond with constructive comments about the content of the text. Suggest that listeners phrase their feedback in terms like these:

   ☀ I liked your dynamic beginning, when you said _____.

   ☀ I liked your tie-up ending because _____.

☀ I liked your word usage because _____.

☀ When you said _____, it reminded me of _____.

☀ When you said _____, it made me feel _____!

☀ As they gain more writing experience, the writers themselves can begin to ask for feedback or advice. They should ask questions like:

Was there anything in my text that you wanted to know more about?

Was there anything that didn't make a clear mental picture in your mind?

5. Be sure that students realize that after the reading and the feedback, the writer deserves a gracious round of applause. This is part of the way the class will learn to celebrate authorship.

Second Revision

Major Goals and Tasks

Second revision provides the writer with an opportunity to make changes that refine the quality of the snapshot.

The writer might describe this phase in these words:

"I am going to reread my snapshot to find out if I need to make changes that will improve the quality of how it sounds and what it says. I'm going to make sure that my snapshot includes:

- all components—who (physical characteristics, personality, feelings), where, when, and what's going on

- a fully-focused topic (a small scenario in time)

- a logical order

- interesting, exceptional language that is not overdone

- a dynamic beginning and a tie-up ending

- varied sentence structure, and complex and interesting sentences."

Background Information and Teaching Tips

1. The brevity of the snapshot text permits students to approach each second revision task with increased confidence. In addition, the process itself—the previous phases they have worked through—has supported them in their work. Thus, they are now in a good position to address refinement. For example, if the coaching session was constructive, many of the second revision tasks have been discussed already, and problem spots have been addressed and changed earlier, in the planning phase. During a successful drafting phase, writers will have focused already upon the content of the text. This means that by now, they will have thought about and developed some of the details to be addressed during second revision.

2. Lesson 13 (pages 66–71) includes directions for introducing second revision tasks to students. However, since providing students with all five tasks at once is a bit overwhelming, Lesson 13 addresses only tasks 1 and 5. Those tasks, as well as the three other second revision tasks, are presented in their entirety on the following pages. As your students become more experienced with the snapshot experience and the writing process, you can ask them to address an increasing number of second revision tasks at one sitting. You can use the tasks on the next two pages as an extension of the Lesson 13 Study Sheet.

Second Revision: A Writer/Coach Discussion

Name _____   Date _____

DIRECTIONS: Listed below are the five revision tasks to be completed during Second Revision. Read your snapshot aloud to a coach. You and your coach should evaluate your writing by talking through each revision task. You can make the necessary revisions to your snapshot as you go along or directly afterward. Then switch coach and writer roles and repeat.

Use a different colored pen or pencil to make your second revisions. If you make any lengthy changes to your text, you might not have enough space within the text to write the revisions. So, organize your revisions in one of the following two ways:

a. Write the changes on sticky notes and attach them to the spot in your text; or

b. Write an asterisk (*) next to the word where the revision begins. On a separate sheet of paper, write an asterisk (*) and the revision you want to make. For the next revision, write **, and on that same sheet of paper, skip a space, mark two asterisks (**) and write out your revision. Continue to use sets of asterisks (***; ****; and so on) for your subsequent revisions.

SECOND REVISION TASKS

1. Fully-Focused Topic

☀ Tell your coach the topic of your snapshot. Then, read your snapshot aloud and ask, "Is there any information that doesn't belong with my topic?" If so, cross out this information.

2. Clearly-Expressed Content

☀ Ask your coach, "Is everything clear?" If something isn't clear, your coach will not be able to form a mental image or sketch the idea.

Here are some other questions that you can ask your coach to help you make the content clear:

"Is anything in my text that is not clear to you or that would not be clear to another reader? Is there something I know a lot about but have not explained well enough?"

"Do my ideas make pictures in your mind? Will you sketch my text?"

☀ As the writer, you should ask yourself, "Does my coach's sketch show all components?" If it doesn't, you need to make the necessary revisions to your snapshot so that all components are represented.

Second Revision: A Writer/Coach Discussion

Name _____   Date _____

3. Exceptional Word Choice

☀ Read your text to your coach and ask, "Are my words interesting? Does my text include high-imagery language? Did I use a simile or a metaphor that catches your attention?" If not, figure out where in your text you can change the writing to add interest and imagery.

4. Logical/Sequential Order with Smooth Transitions

☀ Cut your text apart, sentence by sentence. Place the strips on your desk in the order you wrote them, and ask yourself if the events are in a logical order.

☀ Read the text aloud to your coach and ask, "Does my text make sense to you? Is it in logical order?" If not, move the ideas around until they do make sense.

☀ Finally, read your text to your coach and ask, "Can you easily follow along from one event to the next? If not, what sentence or sentences can I add to make sure the events hang together in a sequential, easy-to-understand way?" If you need to add sentences, write them on strips of paper and place them in your text. Tape or glue your text onto a plain sheet of paper, then copy or type the whole snapshot, being sure to include any changes you made in Steps 1 through 3, as well.

5. Varied Sentence Structure and Complex Sentences

☀ Ask your coach:

"Does each sentence start the same way? Are my sentences too simple and boring?" For example:

I went to the movie with my friend. I sat in the first row. I like to see the movie up close.

☀ If so, can you and your coach figure out how to change one or two of the sentences? For example:

My friend and I went to the movie and sat in the first row. Huge! That's how the characters in the movie looked because we were sitting so close to the screen. I liked the huge look of everything and the gigantic sound!

Make all changes to your snapshot so that your second revision is now complete.

Editing

Major Goals and Tasks

During the editing phase, the writer has the opportunity to correct conventional mistakes such as punctuation, spelling, capitalization, and subject/verb agreement.

The writer might describe this phase in these words:

> "I am going to reread my snapshot to correct for:
> - capitalization at the beginning of sentences
> - capitalization of proper nouns (also the personal pronoun I)
> - end-of-sentence and middle-of-sentence punctuation
> - subject/verb agreement within my sentences and paragraphs
> - run-on sentences or sentence fragments, and
> - misspelled words."

Background Information and Teaching Tips

1. The term *editing* refers to the tasks a writer performs to prepare a grammatically correct text. When a text is grammatically correct, we say it is *conventional* (standard; usual and expected). Grammatical tasks are often called *conventions*. Statewide writing assessments commonly hold students accountable for capitalization, punctuation (both within and at the end of sentences), paragraphing, subject/verb agreement, spelling, and legibility. When learning to deal with these editing tasks, it's important that a writer concentrate on one at a time. For example, a writer should learn to edit for capital letters, rereading the text once through for the sole purpose of identifying any errors in capital letter usage. Thus, a writing assignment will be edited several times, each time for a different convention. Over time, as your students gain more control over each task, they will learn to multi-task. But when beginning, having them edit one task at a time is the best approach.

    A writer's fundamental purpose is to convey meaning to the reader. Before students begin the editing phase, remind them that although we tend to think that our use of words in sentences and paragraphs is the only means of conveying meaning, conventions such as punctuation are also used to accomplish this goal. For example, if a writer wishes to convey emotional excitement with words, he or she might place an exclamation mark at the end of the sentence. Punctuation marks, therefore, help convey the meaning.

2. Teaching students about conventions from this functional perspective increases their ability to be independent and decreases their reliance upon grades or verbal prodding to improve their writing. Therefore, providing students with strategies that support their understanding of an editing task should be the focal point of this phase. If students acquire the reasoning skills fostered by a strategy, you won't have to rerun a mini-lesson multiple times. For instance, after a solid introduction of an editing strategy focused on correct use of capital letters, followed by one or two well-structured mini-lessons, students should be able to handle the editing tasks independently. They should be able by then to trust themselves to understand the logic of capital letters.

   In classrooms where the writing program offers frequent and authentic opportunities for formal and informal publication, students will be more likely to become competent writers. When they know that their writing will be published, students try hard to use conventions that assist in conveying precise meaning. In such environments, when a student is asked why he or she learns to edit, a common response is: "I study the rules because I want to make my text clear for my readers." In a classroom where students have little opportunity to publish, common responses to the same question are, "My teacher makes me," or "Well, because I have to."

3. Using a short text such as a snapshot to teach editing strategies gives you a number of options. Because these mini-lessons are short and to the point, you can either teach one or two editing strategies during the first snapshot assignment, or you may decide to spread the editing lessons between the second and third snapshot assignments. (Naturally, if your students have not been taught a particular editing strategy yet, they should not be expected to edit the text for that element.) Make clear to students that once they have learned all of the strategies, they will be expected to assume responsibility for all editing tasks.

4. If you choose to publish a snapshot before all editing mini-lessons have been taught, the text can be sent for final editing to an "outside editor" (you and/or a small group of students). After the outside editor provides feedback (usually via standard proofreading marks, which should be reviewed), the text is returned to the writer for final correction. When a writer is editing his or her own work, it is not necessary to use standard proofreading marks. Students can simply cross out an error and make the correction above the error. It's preferable to cross out, rather than erase an error because this will enable you to examine a series of drafts for evidence of improvement.

5. During the editing phase, encourage students to think of themselves as inquirers and researchers. Make available a collection of reference materials in the

classroom. Writers need access to more resources than their grammar textbooks and the usual set of classroom dictionaries. Different kinds of dictionaries—a dictionary of names, a spelling dictionary, a specialized dictionary like a science dictionary, and a thesaurus—are each valuable to have on hand for writers. Try to make available, as well, other resources such as a gazetteer, an atlas, maps, and a phone book. The References (pages 141–144) provide specific recommendations.

Ultimately the goal is for each writer to become an independent problem solver. For this reason, the strategies included in the editing lessons are meant to be problem-solving devices. The strategies cover capitalization, punctuation, and spelling. Because spelling is frequently a particularly sticky problem for students, some of the more common concerns are briefly addressed below.

The Special Dilemma of Spelling Instruction

When writers begin drafting, a predictable clamor often arises. Some students call aloud, "I don't know how to spell _____." This distracts all the writers from the weighty task of getting ideas down on paper. Almost reflexively you, the caring teacher, rush to the rescue.

Your "teacher rescue response" has wedged you between a rock and a hard place. You can rush to the rescue if you choose, but remember that when you tell a writer how to spell a word, the information travels in one ear and right out the other. Although under certain rare circumstances, simply telling the student the correct spelling is the right thing to do, typically it is an instructional dead end.

To extricate yourself from this dilemma, you might ask yourself, "What does a writer really mean when she or he clamors, 'I don't know how to spell ____!'" Here are some possibilities:

☀ I'm emotionally distraught!

☀ I'm in a failure situation.

☀ I'm scared to take a risk to put anything down on paper.

☀ If I call out, my teacher will rush to the rescue, and then I'll be off the hook.

☀ I don't have a strategy to dig myself out of this mess!

The two Think-It-Through spelling strategies in Lesson 12 (pages 63–65) are designed to enhance a writer's thinking and confidence. The second strategy, "From Problem Solving to Trusting Yourself," is especially valuable for building confidence. Recall that the strategy places students in a small study group that deals only with spelling. Each group member assumes a role: leader, researcher, or speller. The speller solves problems, recalling known phonetic, visual, or auditory information, while his or her classmates support the inquiry. Classmates encourage the speller, reminding him or her, "You should trust yourself. You know more than you think you know."

Teachers who have participated in staff development with the author, and who have chosen to use "From Problem Solving to Trusting Yourself" on a consistent basis, report that students gain confidence and that during drafting they stop asking for the teacher's help. Also, if the teacher has focused on the basic sight words, requiring groups of students to study them, the words begin to show up correctly spelled even in drafts.

Remember (and remind students, too) that even though students do not have access to a dictionary during statewide testing, they do have access to the thinking skills and knowledge stored within themselves. With a resource like the Think-It-Through spelling strategies, students can learn to function more effectively under the pressure of testing.

Formal Publication and Evaluation

Major Goals and Tasks

Formal publication offers the writer the opportunity to go public with his or her snapshot. As writers realize that they usually will not be present to clarify their message for readers, they will strive to get the content and conventions correct.

The writer might describe this phase in these words:

> "I am going to put my snapshot into a book for others to read. I want my readers to think my snapshot is well-crafted. I want my readers to think I am a competent writer and enjoy my writing."

Background Information and Teaching Tips

1. Without publication opportunities, a writing program is unlikely to succeed. An effective writing program includes two forms of publication, informal and formal.

   As discussed earlier, through informal publication, writers find out if their intended message is being communicated, and they have an early opportunity to receive feedback for revision.

   Formal publication is a very different experience. At this point, the writer prepares the text for readers, knowing that he or she will probably not be present when the text is read. The opportunity to solicit immediate feedback is not possible. A formally published text must impress the reader with a clear, meaningful message, and it must be conventionally correct in terms of capital letter usage, punctuation, subject-verb agreement, and spelling. The quality of a formally published text reflects directly upon the credibility of the writer.

2. Some teachers consider publication to be too time-consuming. However, regular language arts class periods can be devoted to the core curriculum tasks that involve reading, listening, speaking, thinking, writing, grammar, spelling, and computer usage—all elements of publishing. The final touches to a publication can be made simple and brief. For instance, "book binding" can mean simply stapling the final papers together or placing them in a three-ringed binder.

And there are multiple possibilities for formal publication: personal letters sent to far-away readers; original stories assembled in a book; public and personal messages placed on a message board; classroom newspapers; or written snapshots placed in a classroom collection that can be sent home to parent and grandparent readers, and placed in the school library. Remember, the pay-off of formal publication is great. Writers experience the pleasure of knowing their work is actually being read; of having the satisfaction of seeing a process through to the end; and of witnessing a product of their own creation come into being.

A Natural Step: Applying Snapshot Writing Knowledge to the Longer Text of the State Writing Assessment

Snapshot Knowledge and a Longer Text

 N THE PROCESS OF LEARNING HOW TO WRITE A WELL-CRAFTED SNAPSHOT, writers have gained considerable confidence as well as a wealth of knowledge. For example, snapshot writers now know how to:

- ☀ select a topic and narrow the time frame of the content
- ☀ plan a text by thinking and talking through it (paired or self-coaching)
- ☀ write a well-crafted text according to state rubric descriptors
- ☀ apply all phases of the writing process
- ☀ reflect (debrief) and figure out how to improve

This wealth of knowledge can be applied to the writing of a longer text. Two key snapshot-writing experiences can help students make the transfer from the snapshot assignment to longer text:

☀ the transition experience from paired to self-coaching

☀ the coaching experience as a planning/thinking device

From the third snapshot writing assignment on, the lessons encourage a writer's transition from paired coaching to self-coaching. This transition aids the writer in *thinking and talking through* an idea while coaching him or herself, and consequently moves the writer toward independent thinking. During the progression of snapshot assignments it was also suggested that you use the "Writing Coach's Evaluation Checklist of Snapshot Skills" to monitor, evaluate, and debrief the writer. Doing this gives the writer several opportunities to internalize knowledge about what makes a well-crafted text and about the procedure to write a well-crafted text. The ability to self-coach will help students not only to prepare for the statewide writing prompt, but more importantly, it will enhance all their future writing experiences, in school and in their careers.

The second transferable snapshot experience is the coaching session itself. From the first snapshot assignment, writers were taught to use the coaching experience as a thinking/planning device. Both your modeling and their own practice with the "Writing Coach's Prompt" (which aligns with the requirements on the state rubric) taught students to *think through, mull over,* and *articulate* ideas.

In essence, the coaching experience is an oral planner. Many state writing assessments provide a planner, but do not include the writer's use of the planner in the scoring. If this is so for you, then you have leeway to devise a planner that will prove most supportive as a thinking device.

Devising and Using a Planner That Supports Thinking

The planner on page 120, "Using Snapshot Knowledge to Plan a Longer Text: Writing Coach or Self-Coach Prompt," is set up like the "Writing Coach's Prompt" that was used in the lessons. The thinking fostered by this planner helps the writer to:

☀ identify story elements—who, where, when, and what's the issue

☀ narrow the time frame the story represents

☀ think and talk through each story section—beginning, middle, and end

☀ identify and describe the snapshots to be used in each section

☀ think and talk through the story to gain flow and clarification of language choices

* figure out a title (often writers don't designate a title until after the text is written)

* jot down content notes (not sentences) in each section (beginning, middle, end)

* sketch camera icons to represent rubric-rich snapshots to be included in each section

A demonstration lesson on teaching students how to plan a longer text is included on pages 115–119. First, however, study the discussion below, which addresses how you can help your students avoid the most common mistake in using planners.

Note-Taking and Snapshot Thinking

Teachers often make the mistake of allowing students to write full sentences on the planner. If students do so, they will most likely transcribe the sentences from the planner onto the writing paper, resulting in a low-scoring text. The planner should serve as a thinking device, not a written text. Students will know how to approach and use a planner correctly if you first model how to jot down notes on it.

Start by telling students that a note written on a planner is merely a word or a phrase that represents a huge, elaborate idea the writer is holding in his or her mind. After a writer has *thought and talked through* a text, he or she jots down notes on the planner to represent these ideas. It is almost as if the planner notes are concrete placeholders for the writer's thoughts. A writer can sketch a small snapshot icon (a camera) next to the note to represent the huge idea that is in his or her mind. A writer rarely, if ever, puts full sentences on the planner. Those full sentences will be put down on paper during drafting.

Use a transparency of the "Planner and Snapshot Thinking" (page 122) to demonstrate the example below. Informing students, "Here's the "Beginning" section of a planner—with notes and snapshot icons—for a story."

Beginning

* on family vacation (who, where, when, and what's the issue)

* never seen the ocean before 📷

* ran into the water 📷

Highlight the writer's notes, pointing out, "The 'Beginning' section of this writer's planner looks like a few words with snapshot icons beside each idea. Because the writer has been coached or coached himself through his plan, the huge ideas were kept in his mind. I'll read the writer's final text for the beginning of his story. You listen and see if you can match the writer's notes with his text."

We'd been driving for two full days. Mom, Dad, and I were getting cranky from being in the car all that time. We were on a family vacation and finally had arrived in Fernandina Beach! This was the first time I'd ever seen the ocean, and my brain was running like a cheetah trying to imagine what it would be like. So, we were driving down the road heading straight for the beach, and it looked like the road just ran off into the sky. But no, it was the ocean, the real, honest ocean. Dad parked the car, and I ran like a crazy man right onto the beach. I couldn't believe my eyes or my ears! It looked like the ocean went on forever, and it sounded like the roar of a million voices. I threw off my shoes. The sand felt like sun fire, so I dashed into the surf. The wave crashed right on me, knocking me down. Mom and Dad just stood there watching and laughing.

Ask your students to look again at the writer's notes. After you re-read the text to them, ask them something like, "How do you think the writer was able to jot down notes and snapshot icons, and then come up with such a fluent beginning for his story?" (From their snapshot experiences, students should be able to explain that the writer has used a coach or self-coached to *think and talk through* the text.) Then ask students to identify the writer's exceptional language. Point out that none of that language was written on the planner; instead, the coaching session had been effective, and therefore the writer had mentally formed a well-crafted snapshot. Inform students that a reader knows if the writer's planning session was carefully done because the text will include well-developed, rubric-rich snapshots. In short, the reader will know if the writer knows how to apply snapshot thinking.

The most effective way to teach note-taking and snapshot thinking is to model the process. The demonstration lesson on pages 115–119 provides a script from which you can model how to think through, mull ideas, organize ideas into snapshots, and jot down notes on a planner. You can use the example as your demonstration lesson or design one of your own.

A Demonstration Lesson

PREPARING FOR THE LESSON

☀ A well-chosen photo is a good springboard for narrowing in on and selecting a topic. You might use the one from the Lesson 1 Study Sheet, "Snapshot Components," along with the script provided in this Demonstration Lesson, or you might choose a photo of your own and write a script to match it. If you use your own photo, make sure that the content of the photo reflects information about who, where, when, and what's going on.

☀ Make an overhead transparency of the blank form, "Planner and Snapshot Thinking," and have available a copy of "Planner and Snapshot Thinking: Teacher's Answers" (page 121).

☀ Make a copy for each student of "Using Snapshot Knowledge to Plan a Longer Text: Writing Coach or Self-Coach Prompt" (page 120). Also, make a transparency for your own use.

☀ Give each student a copy of the story, *Midnight and the Miracle Additive* found on page 123. Or, if you have prepared a demonstration model of your own, make a copy for each student of your final publication.

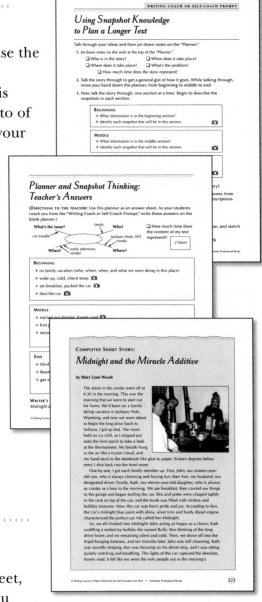

PRESENTING THE LESSON

Selecting a Topic (narrowing the time frame)

1 Give each student a copy of the Lesson 1 Study Sheet, "Snapshot Components" or a copy of the photo you selected. Explain that a snapshot can be a starter for a longer story. If you choose to use the Lesson 1 Study Sheet, use the following script. If you choose your own snapshot, use this script as a model to design your own script. During your presentation of either script, use a think-aloud process in which you pause and demonstrate mulling over your thoughts as you come up with this plan.

> *This is a snapshot taken on a family vacation, and I want to write a short story about that vacation. If I try to write about the whole vacation, it will be too much information to handle in a short story. So, I need to narrow the topic.*

Hmmmmm… I think I'll write about what happened on the morning we started for home. Yes, that morning was an intense thriller! I can really weave a great tale about it. That morning's thrill took about, hmmmmmm, two hours. Hmmmm, yes, what I want to write about is that wild and tense two hours. Yes, from start to finish, that event was about two hours.

Planning

2 Distribute to each student a copy of "Using Snapshot Knowledge to Plan a Longer Text: Writing Coach or Self-Coach Prompt." Place your transparency of the blank "Planner and Snapshot Thinking" on the overhead. (As you continue through the planning phases, keep your copy of the "Planner and Snapshot Thinking: Teacher's Answers" handy. As your students coach you throughout this planning session, the "Teacher's Answers" sheet can serve as the guide to what you fill in on the blank "Planner" transparency.) The script just below illustrates one possible way you might address students as you model.

First I will jot down notes to fill in the web at the top of the planner. I need to include notes for this information: who, where, when, what's the issue, and how much time my story represents.

I must remember to use notes throughout. The planner is not the place for writing full sentences. I'll write full sentences during drafting.

Next, just like planning a snapshot, I need to think and talk through my plan. If I do this during planning, later—when I am drafting—the writing will flow more easily from my head to the paper.

For now, until I am secure enough to coach myself, I'd like you to be my writing coaches. Since both you and I have a lot experience writing snapshots, I'm sure that after one coaching session with you, I should be able to coach myself. I believe that will be true for you, too.

3 Ask students to browse through Items 2 through 6 on the "Prompt" sheet, paying particular attention to Items 2, 3, and 4. Point out that in each one of these steps, students will be asking you to think and talk through your text.

The first *think and talk through*, Item 2, is short and general so the writer can get an overall sense of his or her story. Point out to students that as you talk through your story, you'll be moving your hand down the planner from the beginning section to the middle section to the end. Explain that the physical action of *place holding* the events in the story helps you organize your thoughts and language choices. Inform students that you will not write anything on the planner until you get to Item 6 on the "Prompt" sheet. For now, you will just talk, think, and move your hand. Then, follow this script or your own script as students prompt you for Item 2.

Well, first I got up. We were in a condo near Jackson Hole, Wyoming. It was early and very cold. I went outside to check the temperature. Then I got everybody up and we ate our breakfast. We packed the car and started out. Then the car trouble began. Everybody got real scared. Kath really lost it. I think there were two times when the car—oh yeah, Ken called the car Midnight. There were, hmmmmmm, three times when Midnight jerked and jolted. Then she straightened out. When we finally got to a gas station, the guy said all we needed was an additive.

4 Ask students to continue to coach you now through the first part of Item 3. Repeat to them that moving your hand down the blank planner is important because you are relying on action to help organize your thinking. Follow this script or your own:

Well, I got up real early, about 4:30 in the morning. Man, it was cold. When I went out on the porch to check the temperature, it was so cold that I could see my breath in the air. My hand stuck to the doorknob.

Then I got everybody up. John is real easy to get up because he is so happy, always clowning! Ken was to do the driving, and I knew he'd be sleepy. Kath is cranky in the mornings. It's not fun to get her up. We ate our breakfast, then went to the garage to pack the car. Ken loved that car. It was midnight blue with silver trim and had a diesel engine. He called it Midnight. He thought it was the perfect car. So, we climbed into the car. It was really dark and cold outside. John was still clowning. Kath had her stuffed buffalo that she'd bought at a gift shop. She named him Buffy. Ken was our serious driver. I remember being quiet and cold.

Then, it all started. The car jerked, lurched forward and slowed down. John got quiet, Kath woke up scared, Ken got tense, and I think I stopped breathing. Yes, that's what happened. Then the car smoothed out and everybody went back to what they'd been doing. John started clowning, Kath and the buffalo went back to sleep, Ken relaxed, and I started breathing, and oh, Midnight went on down the road.

Then, the same thing happened again. Midnight jerked and jolted and slowed down. Everybody reacted the same, but worse than the first time. Then Midnight smoothed out and everybody relaxed.

Then, it happened again. This time everybody got frantic, especially Kath. She started screaming about how she was going to die and all her friends would never see her again. Ken's shoulders and neck got really tense. John stopped clowning, and I stopped breathing. Then, there was this loud BOOM! I saw a trail of smoke coming out of the exhaust pipe. Then Midnight smoothed out, and luckily we got to a gas station. The man said that the fuel line was frozen and all we needed was an additive. He said that diesel engines do that. He said we were really lucky that we didn't get stuck out on the road in this cold weather.

5 Now ask students to coach you through the second part of Item 3: "Have you (I) identified the beginning, middle, and end of the story?" Follow this script or your own. Place your hand on the beginning section of the planner.

> *Yes, I know that the beginning tells:*
>   * ☀ *who, where, when, what we are doing in this place*
>   * ☀ *about waking up and how cold it was*
>   * ☀ *how we ate breakfast and packed the car*
>   * ☀ *I want to describe the car and tell how Ken thought it was the perfect car*

Place your hand on the middle section of the planner.

> *Then, in the middle it tells*
>   * ☀ *how we got started and how lonely and deserted the road was*
>   * ☀ *then first jerk and smooth out and how everybody reacted*
>   * ☀ *second jerk and smooth out and how everybody reacted*

Finally, place your hand on the end section of the planner.

> *And in the end*
>   * ☀ *third jerk and how everybody reacted*
>   * ☀ *the big boom and how everybody reacted*
>   * ☀ *getting to the gas station and what the man told us*

6 Ask students to listen while you think and talk through Item 4. This time instead of following a prepared script, use your own language knowledge to elaborate the demonstration story or your own story. As you do so, you'll find that the first two *think and talk through* experiences have set you up to generate a logically ordered, language rich elaboration. It's okay during planning to indicate that you aren't totally sure how you want to express an idea, and that you will continue to think about it when you jot down notes on the planner and even while drafting.

Next, have students ask you the question at the end of Item 4. Using the "Planner and Snapshot Thinking: Teacher's Answers," tell students approximately how many snapshots are in each section. It's still okay to think and mull over ideas; for example, you might say, "Well, yes, hmmmm, I will figure this snapshot out when I jot down the notes on the planner."

7 For Item 5, you might tell students that you have already figured out your title, or you might decide to tell them you'll figure out the title only after the story is written. It is not uncommon for an author to designate the title after a text is written.

8 For Item 6, you can use your copy of the "Planner and Snapshot Thinking: Teacher's Answers" as the source for jotting down notes on the blank planner. Some writers insert the snapshot icon as they make each note; others insert it after jotting down the notes for one whole section. Either way is fine, as long as it supports the writer's planning process.

9   Debrief with your students. Pose questions like:

☀ *What have you learned about how to plan a longer text?*

☀ *What have you learned about jotting down notes and planning snapshots?*

☀ *What are your questions and comments?*

10   Give each student the final copy of the text, *Midnight and the Miracle Additive,* or of your own text. Read the text aloud. Place the "Planner and Snapshot Thinking" sheet with your notes on the overhead. Ask students to share their thoughts with a partner about what the writer did and thought to get from the notes on the planner to the final version.

Using Snapshot Knowledge to Plan a Longer Text

Talk through your ideas and then jot down notes on the "Planner."

1. Jot down notes on the web at the top of the "Planner."

❏ Who is in the story? ❏ When does it take place?

❏ Where does it take place? ❏ What's the problem?

❏ How much time does the story represent?

2. Talk the story through to get a general gist of how it goes. While talking through, move your hand down the planner, from beginning to middle to end.

3. Now, talk the story through, one section at a time. Begin to describe the snapshots in each section.

BEGINNING

☀ What information is in the beginning section?

☀ Identify each snapshot that will be in this section.

MIDDLE

☀ What information is in the middle section?

☀ Identify each snapshot that will be in this section.

END

☀ What information is in the end section?

☀ Identify each snapshot that will be in this section.

❏ Have you (I) identified the beginning, middle, and end of the story?

4. Talk the story through for the last time. Move your hand down the planner, from beginning to middle to end, this time talking through the snapshot descriptions planned for each section.

❏ How many snapshots are in each section?

5. Have you (I) figured out a title for the story?

6. Jot down notes (not sentences) in each section as reminders of the plan, and sketch a camera as a reminder of the snapshots planned for each section.

7. ❏ Drafting ❏ First Revision ❏ Second Revision ❏ Editing

Planner and Snapshot Thinking: Teacher's Answers

(**DIRECTIONS TO THE TEACHER:** Use this planner as an answer sheet. As your students coach you from the "Writing Coach or Self-Coach Prompt," write these answers on the blank planner.)

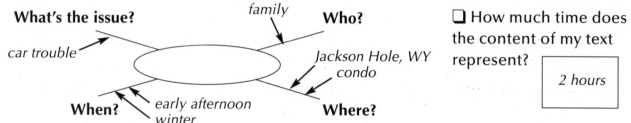

What's the issue?

car trouble

family

Who?

Jackson Hole, WY condo

When?

early afternoon
winter

Where?

☐ How much time does the content of my text represent?

2 hours

BEGINNING

☀ on family vacation (who, where, when, and what we were doing in this place)

☀ woke up, cold, check temp. 📷

☀ ate breakfast, packed the car 📷

☀ describe car 📷

MIDDLE

☀ started out driving, lonely road 📷

☀ first jerk 📷

☀ second jerk 📷

END

☀ third jerk 📷

☀ Boom! 📷

☀ gas station and what man said 📷

WRITER'S QUESTION AND ANSWER: Have I figured out a title? Yes!
Midnight and the Miracle Additive

Planner and Snapshot Thinking

What's the issue?　　　　**Who?**

When?　　　　**Where?**

❑ How much time does
the content of my text
represent?

BEGINNING

MIDDLE

END

Midnight and the Miracle Additive

by Mary Lynn Woods

The alarm in the condo went off at 4:30 in the morning. This was the morning that we were to start out for home. We'd been on a family skiing vacation in Jackson Hole, Wyoming, and now we were about to begin the long drive back to Indiana. I got up first. The room held an icy chill, so I slipped out onto the front porch to take a look at the thermometer. My breath hung in the air like a frozen cloud, and

my hand stuck to the doorknob like glue to paper. Sixteen degrees below zero! I shot back into the front room.

One-by-one, I got each family member up. First, John, our sixteen-year-old son, who is always clowning and having fun; then Ken, my husband, our designated driver. Finally, Kath, our eleven-year-old daughter, who is always as cranky as a bear in the morning. We ate breakfast, then carried our things to the garage and began stuffing the car. Skis and poles were clasped tightly in the rack on top of the car, and the trunk was filled with clothes and holiday treasures. Now, this car was Ken's pride and joy. According to Ken, the car's midnight blue paint with shiny, silver trim and hardy diesel engine characterized the perfect car. He called her *Midnight.*

So, we all climbed into *Midnight:* John acting as happy as a clown; Kath cuddling a stuffed toy buffalo she named Buffy; Ken thinking of the long drive home; and me remaining silent and cold. Then, we drove off into the frigid-hanging darkness, and ten minutes later, John was still clowning, Kath was soundly sleeping, Ken was focusing on his driver-ship, and I was sitting quietly watching and breathing. The lights of the car captured the desolate, lonely road. It felt like we were the only people out in the morning's numbness. A sign whisked by that said something like—no town for the next 20 miles. I settled into the rhythm of my breathing.

Then jolt! The car lurched forward, then slowed to a crawl! John stopped clowning! Kath woke up startled and whimpering. Ken's shoulders pulled tense and tight. I held my breath, and then, *Midnight* smoothed out and moved forward at her usual speed. John started clowning. Kath went back to sleep. Ken's shoulders relaxed. I returned to my breathing, and *Midnight* glided down the road.

Then jerk! The car lurched forward again, then slowed to a creeping crawl! John stopped clowning. Kath woke up shrieking and clinging to the stuffed buffalo. Ken's shoulders and neck tightened like a rope during tug of war. I stopped breathing, and then, *Midnight* smoothed out and moved forward at her old speed. John started clowning. Kath went back to sleep. Ken's shoulders relaxed. I resumed breathing, and *Midnight* glided down the road.

Then jolt, jerk, jolt! *Midnight* lurched forward then slowed to a turtle-paced crawl! John stopped clowning. Kath woke up frantically waving Buffy in the air, and screaming that she didn't want to die on this lonely road because her friends would never get to see her again. The tension crept into Ken's shoulders and neck like a strangling vine. I thought I'd never take another breath, and then, *BOOM*! A blast burst from the exhaust pipe, and as I turned to look through the rear window, I saw a cloud of smoke trail off into the morning's dawn. Then, *Midnight* lurched forward and smoothed out. A road sign whisked by that said something calming like the next town was five miles ahead. John started clowning. Kath and the buffalo lapsed into slumber. The tension uncoiled from Ken's shoulders and neck. I rolled into the rhythm of my breathing, and within ten minutes, *Midnight* rolled into a gas station.

"Yep, that's what I thought," the station attendant said as he pulled himself out from under the hood. "Sure enough! Your fuel line is frozen! That's the thing with a diesel engine! It's a miracle the car didn't just stop dead out there on the road! I'll give her a drink of this additive! That'll do her! Won't be but a minute, and you'll be on the road with no problems!"

One Fifth-Grade Classroom Example: *Writing Snapshots and Preparing Students for the State Writing Assessment*

Following is an extended example of a fifth-grade teacher's experience as she engaged her class in snapshot writing and as she prepared them for the Indiana state writing assessment.

Kelly Wilson's Fifth-Grade Experience with Writing Snapshots*

TEACHER'S REFLECTIONS

In the fall, I began by teaching my students how to write snapshots, how to improve coaching skills, and eventually how to make the transition to the writing of a longer text, a memoir. Finally, I made the leap into teaching the students how to write to a prompt and how to manage the state assessment time factor. Throughout this progression of events, my students and I used *debriefing* as a means of finding out what we'd learned and what actions we needed to take to resolve problems.

Initially, the thought of teaching them how to apply all phases of the authoring process—selecting a topic, planning, drafting, first and second revision, editing, and publishing—sent me into big time stress. On top of all of this, I had expectations that exceeded the test. I wanted my students to learn to write for their own needs, and yes, I wanted them to like it. For myself, I wanted to find out how to teach writing and to feel prepared to do it. This year I have 23 fifth graders, 14 boys and 9 girls. How would all of this be possible?

The amazing thing is that as we all learned what we needed to know to improve, we *did* improve. And then, as we felt ourselves getting better, this very feeling began to lower the stress—mine and my students'.

Following the snapshot instruction and the focused instruction on coaching skills, I felt the students needed continuous experience writing, so one hour daily was set aside for writing instruction. We moved on to the longer text of the memoir, and after that to texts based on students' own choices. At first we worked through the writing process together, step-by-step, but as the class progressed, students began to take more responsibility independently.

During the hourly writing sessions, I was able to pull small groups together and base the mini-lesson upon individual or group needs. For example, I showed one group examples of how a published author uses snapshots to attract and hold a reader's attention, consequently establishing *voice* for the text. Because each student knew so much about writing a well-crafted snapshot by then, it was easy to build and improve skills. I began to treat each student like a real writer, and soon group conferences shifted from my solo talk to discussions. Each student's memoirs and personal choice texts began to show improvement.

Eventually during our writer's workshop, my job was to read first drafts. I decided that the time had come to assume the role of *outside editor*. I focused upon the content and conventions separately. To focus on content, I used red pen to mark the drafts—inserting a camera icon to indicate a reader's need for a snapshot, and/or a question

* Kelly Wilson, fifth-grade teacher, Central Elementary School, Lebanon, Indiana

mark to indicate a reader's need for clarity or exceptional word usage. I wasn't sure how the students would react to my red-pen markings. Much to my relief, the students were at ease with my markings and went about making second revisions with enthusiasm. They did not feel criticized, but rather they felt in control. They knew what to do, and I celebrated their independence.

I have selected three writing samples to share here. I could have chosen any number from the many excellent samples written in my classroom; it was very difficult to select just three. Each of those selected was written by a student who achieved significant progress. These samples thus reflect a major degree of improvement and control over the content portion of the state rubric; these students exceeded my expectations, and most certainly their own.

The first sample is Whitney's memoir. I have included her planner, red-penned draft, and final paper. I selected her work because it clearly shows her to be an independent writer who understands how to create a well-crafted text and manage the phases of the writing process.

Student Work Samples: Whitney's Planner

BEGINNING

* hot day (12:30 P.M.)
* by statue
* Daniel says
* us looking for him

MIDDLE

* Grandma finds him
* shirt
* no one tells and walks into the Capitol
* mad!

END

* we laugh
* then go shop

The Unpleasant Surprise
by Whitney

(red-penned draft)

It was a hot July day so hot that when you walked your feet burned. I was in Washington D.C. with: my mom, dad, brother, grandma, grandpa, aunt and uncle and three kids, and my other aunt and uncle and their daughter.

We were standing by the UGLY statue 📷 it was uglier than a shaved cat! We had been taking a rest because we had walked for about 3 hours! My cousin Daniel thought he would be funny **(?)** and go hide, he told me and that was it.

After about 5 minutes we decided to head for the Capitol Building. My dad took count and noticed that Daniel was missing. We looked and looked for him. My grandma happened to see his bright yellow shirt under a tree. We were glad we could get going again!

We started to walk and my cousin saw something white on Daniel's shirt. He said, "Look Whit **(?)** at Daniel's shirt." I laughed. We said nothing.

After we got into the beautiful Capitol Building Daniel looked over his left shoulder and smelt something awful. He saw the unpleasant surprise on his shirt. 📷 I laughed so hard I thought my jaw would fall off. My grandpa said "That's what you get for hiding under a tree with birds!"

He got so mad I thought he was going to bust! His face was reder than a firetruck! He made us leave and go buy a new shirt. That was a day I will never forget.

The Unpleasant Surprise
by Whitney

(final copy)

It was a boiling hot July day, so hot that when I walked it felt like my feet were burning! Ouch! I was in Washington, D.C. with my mom, dad, brother, grandma, grandpa, my two aunts and uncles, and three cousins. Daniel, my funny guy teenage cousin, had his girlfriend with him.

We were taking a break by this statue of a man flexing his muscles. This cream colored man was leaning on a horse. He was extremely ugly! Daniel named him, *Ugly Hercules* because he was ugly, if not uglier than a shaved cat!

We were standing by *Ugly Hercules* because we had been sightseeing for about three hours. I looked over, and to my surprise I saw Daniel with a cruel smile. He looked like an evil witch with a horrible idea. Daniel signaled me over. He told me he was going to go hide and not to tell anyone.

After about ten minutes we decided to head for the Capitol Building. My dad took count and noticed that Daniel was missing. We looked for what seemed like two hours, but was really only fifteen minutes. Then, my grandma happened to notice a bright yellow shirt under a tree.

We were all happy we could get moving again! So we started to walk and my cousin Kent hollered, "Whitney, come here! Look at Daniel's shirt!" I laughed quietly, but didn't say anything.

After we got into the beautiful Capitol, Daniel looked over his left shoulder and smelled something awful. He saw a big blob of unpleasant white surprise! My grandma said, "Daniel, that's what you get for hiding under a tree!" Daniel's face made me laugh real loud. I could have sworn my jaw was going to fall off! He turned bright red, as red as a fire truck, and his wicked smile dropped ten feet! After we all had calmed down, he made us go buy him another shirt!

TEACHER'S REFLECTIONS

I knew that I must provide the type of writing experience that my students would encounter on the state writing assessment, so we shifted from snapshots and memoirs to the prompt format. Many teachers prepare students for the state assessment by assigning one prompt every nine weeks, but I knew that this was not going to give my students adequate practice. So, I secured past writing prompts that had been used in our state. Among the prompts I reviewed, I identified three formats: an essay, a how-to, and a short story.

My students and I began to make a classroom rubric for each type and then discussed how we could embed snapshots into the various formats. I asked the students to create prompts for each format so that we would have a collection of prompts from which to write. One hour each week was devoted to practicing for the state writing assessment using the past state prompts and our own. I worked with small groups, highlighting necessary revisions, recommending the editing of conventions, and teaching students how to manage the hour.

Craig was a student who was extremely resistant to writing—even as few as two sentences. I knew that he was the type of learner who had good thoughts, but was hesitant to write something down onto paper. However, that's no longer the case.

I have selected for inclusion here a short story Craig wrote for the story writing prompt. The prompt read: *The library is sponsoring a short story contest. The only rule is that every story must include the following sentence: It was all the fault of the baby elephant.* I believe that the snapshot writing experiences, specifically the coaching and self-coach training, helped create a major shift in Craig's ability and attitude.

After he wrote his draft for the baby elephant prompt, we had a brief conference and made a list of the issues he needed to address. I made four suggestions: 1) all information about the animal's swimming should be together in the same paragraph; 2) story should have a better wrap-up ending; 3) the verb tense usage must make sense and be consistent; and 4) spelling must be correct (I have italicized the four words he did not correct). I instructed Craig to work on one suggestion at a time, and informed him that he was going to do this on his own. His success is quite a celebration.

Student Work Samples

The Baby Elephant's *Disobediance*
by Craig

George is a baby elephant that is about 5 feet tall, and weighs about 80 pounds and can run fast. George lives in Chinaville, New Mexico. *Over night* he planned to break out the next day, so he got ready to put his plan into action.

The next day was so hot, the zoo keepers were sweating buckets of sweat. Then the zoo keepers went about their morning chores and it stayed hot the whole day.

George was ready! He did a hind leg kick and broke out of his cage. George then walked through the zoo like he was the owner. He remembered his plan to get a drink then go swimming.

George then heard a whining from the other animals cages. He saw that they were wanting to go swimming too. George thought, and it took him a long time to

make up his mind. This was his idea. If he set the other animals free, he wouldn't have to hear that whining anymore. So, George did 21 more hind leg kicks, and he got very hot from doing all those hind leg kicks. He was as hot as a burning fire. So, it took him a long time to do all the rest of the hind leg kicks. Then all of the animals went parading right out of the zoo.

When the zoo keepers came back from their lunches, they realized that all the animals were gone. They had *dissapeared!* Then one of the zoo keepers knew where they all went. They ran over the hill and they saw all the animals. The monkeys were swinging from the vines of the trees and cannon balling into the water! The baby elephant belly flopped into the water. It was all the fault of the baby elephant.

Then the zoo keepers looked at each other and the whole club of zoo keepers jumped into the water! They made a huge *tidle* wave! They all swam for the rest of the day. Then the zoo owner showed up. The zoo owner yelled at them in a loud voice and scolded them for not doing what they were supposed to do. Then the zoo owner shrugged, and he himself jumped in. The zoo owner had never had so much fun in his life! He had become a new man, like seeing his whole zoo in a new way. It was all the fault of the baby elephant! Now, is that really a fault?

TEACHER'S REFLECTIONS

Finally, I decided that the students should have experience completing all writing tasks independently, as would be required during the state assessment. I selected an essay format prompt because I think that this type is more difficult to develop than a short story format prompt. The prompt read:

If you could travel back in time or into the future, what time period would you pick and where would you go? For example, you might choose to see live dinosaurs, witness an interesting historical event that took place in Indiana, or visit the first colony of humans on Mars. Write an essay for your teacher explaining the destination and time period you would pick. Give reasons for your choices. Describe some of the things you would see and do.

I decided to share Kyle's text because at the first of the year he was what I would describe as a shy writer. I felt he had ideas and could list them, but his writing lacked vitality and voice. He had been in small group sessions where the students focused on the techniques published writers use to establish voice. I could see that he was beginning to use snapshot knowledge and small group study to improve his writing. This final sample represents Kyle's independent work. Kyle's writing—in contrast to some students who expressed themselves fluently and with a sense of style right from the start—shows marked improvement in dealing with this complex state requirement.

Student Work Samples

My Parents Were Kids
by Kyle

The time period I would like to go to is the 1950. Three reasons why I would do this are to play sports with my Dad when he was a kid, to play with my Mom when she was a kid, and to meet my grandparents on Mom's side of the family.

One day I found a time machine. I got in and typed 1955-1960. When I stepped out I saw my Dad playing basketball. I walked over and said "Can I play?" He said "Sure." So I got to see and play with Dad as a kid. It was real cool like playing with Michael Jordan.

I got back in the time machine. When I got out I saw Mom playing hopscotch with her friends. They said I could play. My Mom smoked me. I got to see and play with my Mom as a kid. I felt like a kid in a candy shop.

I stepped into the time machine. This time when I stepped out I saw my grandparents. They had both died before I was born. I wish they were still alive. I just gave them a great big hug.

I stepped into the time machine for the final time. When I got out this time I saw that it had only taken an hour to see my parents as kids and my grandparents. Don't kids want to see their parents as kids? Don't kids want to see loved ones that have died before they were born or before they could even remember them?

TEACHER'S REFLECTIONS

Following the progression of instruction from snapshots to memoirs to prompts has made me aware of my students' needs and strengths as writers. Everyone in the class made tremendous growth throughout the year. In my opinion, this is the type of constructive growth that makes the students life-long, everyday writers. The hour we spent each day writing was an effective use of instructional time because I was tailoring the instruction to student's specific needs. The students viewed the time as a cooperative learning environment rather than a "have to do" learning experience. By the end of the year, when the hour was up, I had to make them stop writing. Whenever they had extra time, I watched them head straight for their authors' folders. This is what makes me celebrate teaching.

A Scheduling and Management Plan for the State Writing Assessment

 TATE DEPARTMENTS OF EDUCATION THROUGHOUT THE COUNTRY IMPLEMENT the writing assessment in different ways, but many states require a one-hour, one-sitting session. A key aspect to student success on this assessment is a well-developed sense of how to manage the time allotment.

The table on page 131 is a scheduling device that can be used to help students manage the hour-long, statewide writing assignment. In addition to teaching students how to use this scheduling plan, you might also find it beneficial to teach a math lesson about judging the passage of time.

Teaching Students How to Manage the Hour of the State Writing Prompt Assignment

TIME	TASK	THINGS I DO AND ASK MYSELF
2 minutes	**Focus on the Topic**	☀ I will read the prompt, think about the topic, and select a scenario that I can apply to the topic. Then, I'll narrow the time frame of my scenario.
10 minutes	**Prewriting/Planning** What's the issue? Who? When? Where? **BEGINNING** 📷 **MIDDLE** 📷 **END** 📷	☀ Make a quick web to plan: *who is in the story* *where it takes place* *when it takes place* *what is the issue* ☀ How much time does the content of my story represent? ☀ Coach yourself through: *the beginning and all snapshots* *the middle and all snapshots* *the end and all snapshots* ☀ When I think the plan through, I will use exceptional, high-imagery language. ☀ Have I figured out a title?
18–20 minutes	**Sustained Silent Write**	☀ I will write for 18–20 minutes. ☀ I will write my story from my heart so it has lots of interesting ideas and many details. ☀ I will take risks and use exceptional words and high-imagery phrases. ☀ Make a mental note! I will fix my spelling later—during the editing.

TIME	TASK	THINGS I DO AND ASK MYSELF
2 minutes	**First Revision**	☀ Does this sentence make sense? Did I leave any words out? ☀ Did I fix all missing words?
3 minutes	**Second Revision**	☀ Do all my sentences start the same? If so, I will change one or two to vary my sentence structure.

13 minutes	**Editing**
	
	After each editing task is done, I will put a ✔ on each number of the state's Editing Checklist.
	
	<table><tr><td>**EDITING CHECKLIST**
	
	1. Check your capitalization and punctuation.
	
	2. Spell all words correctly.
	
	3. Check for sentence fragments or run-on sentences.
	
	4. Keep verb tense consistent.
	
	5. Make sure subject and verb agree.
	
	6. Use words according to the rules of Standard English.
	
	7. Remember to paragraph correctly.</td></tr></table>
		☀ I'm going to check for:
		
		☀ Capitalization (quickly reread text)
		Did I begin each sentence with a capital letter?
		Did I capitalize proper nouns?
		Did I capitalize the personal pronoun, I?
		
		☀ Punctuation (quickly reread text)
		Did I put the correct punctuation marks at the end of each sentence?
		Did I put the correct punctuation in the middle of each sentence?
		
		☀ Run-On Sentences
		Are any sentences run-on?
		
		☀ Paragraphing
		Do my paragraphs follow my planner?
		Did I indent?
		
		☀ Spelling (quickly reread text)
		Do I recognize any misspelled words?
		Is the word written on the paper or anywhere in the room?
		Can I Think-It-Through? (Trust myself!)
		
		☀ Verb Tense (quickly reread text)
		Is my verb tense consistent?
		
		☀ Subject/Verb Agreement and Other Bad Grammar Choices
		Any violators? (quickly reread text); these are some typical errors:
		  1. we was
		  2. them don't
		  3. we is
		  4. he gots, she gots, I gots
		  5. ain't
		  6. I got no
		  7. me and my friend (etc.)

Content Area Extensions

APPENDIX 1

*Math Lesson: Math Scenarios**

PURPOSE OF THE LESSON

To write a math snapshot that genuinely explains the meaning of the answers and, thus, more truly demonstrates students' real understanding of the problem

PREPARING FOR THE LESSON

☀ Make a copy for each student of the "Phases of the Writing Process" diagram (page 91).

☀ Make a transparency of the two examples given in this lesson.

☀ Have 4" x 6" cards or cut paper available (for draft and final copy).

PRESENTING THE LESSON

1 Inform students that they are going to learn how to write a math snapshot. A math snapshot can be based on an addition, subtraction, multiplication, or division problem. Use your transparency of the examples given in this lesson to help students understand the assignment. Brainstorm criteria for a math snapshot (one 4" x 6" card must have a math problem with the correct answer; the other card should have a text that is interesting to the reader and that includes a simile or metaphor).

2 Give each student two 4" x 6" index cards to use for a draft. Have students write a math problem (addition, subtraction, multiplication, or division) on one of the index cards.

3 Next, ask each student to think about a short scenario involving the numbers in the problem. To begin, they are to think of a one-scenario snapshot. (See Maddie's snapshot as an example.)

4 After each student selects his or her idea, pair students as writer and coach. The coach should listen as the writer talks through the idea, telling who, where, when, and what's going on, and using descriptive language (simile or metaphor). Next, each pair should switch roles and repeat the process.

5 Give each student a copy of the "Phases of the Writing Process" diagram to use as a checklist while working. After a phase is completed, they should check it off:

☀ drafting   ☀ second revision   ☀ formal publication
☀ first revision   ☀ editing   (hand written or computer)

6 Divide the class into small groups with four or five students in each group. Ask them to sit in a circle. Direct the students to place their index cards with the equations face up in the middle of the circle.

7 Each student reads his or her snapshot aloud. The other members of the group listen and identify which of the equations goes with the snapshot that has been read. If the listeners cannot identify the correct equation, or if the writer made an error in computation, the writer will need to engage in second revision and then present the revised snapshot to the group.

8 When first learning to write math snapshots, students should be asked to include only one scenario in their snapshots. As they gain more experience, their snapshots should include two or more possible scenarios. (See Jessica's example below.)

Teacher's Notes: Before we wrote math snapshots, my students could get the correct answer, but did not understand the concept of computational process. In other words, students could compute, but they were often unable to explain the meaning of their answer. Once students learned to write math snapshots, I knew they understood the meaning of the answer. Math snapshots give students the opportunity to make personal connections with concepts and to express their thinking about math. Here are two examples of students' snapshots.

Two Second-Third Grade Students' Math Problem Examples

Example 1:
One-Scenario
Math Snapshot

$$2 + 2 = 4$$

Example 2:
Two-Scenario
Math Snapshot

$$5 \times 3 = 15$$

One-Scenario Math Snapshot (second card) For my birthday I got two cats and two dogs. The cats' fur is as soft as silk and the dogs' fur is a fluffy as a cloud. I'm as happy as a lark because I've got four furry animals.

Maddie

What a surprise! I found three five-dollar bills in my winter coat pocket. I must have left them there last year. Now, I can buy that Barbie I have been wanting. It costs $12.75. Or, I can take my two friends out for pizza. A large pizza costs $12.50. Either way I will have some change left for me. I feel as rich as a millionaire! Should I spend the money on myself or my friends? What do you think I should do?

Jessica

* *Source for this lesson:* Jenny Stapp, transitional grades 2-3 teacher, Metropolitan School District of Pike Township, Fishback Creek Public Academy, Indianapolis, Indiana

Science Lesson: States of Matter*

PURPOSE OF THE LESSON

To help students sharpen their observation skills as they independently apply their knowledge of coaching, write a well-crafted text, and use all tasks within each phase of the writing process

PREPARING FOR THE LESSON

☀ Assemble a beaker of water, a cup of ice cubes, and a pan of steaming water (placed on a burner).

☀ Make a copy for each student of the diagram, "Phases of the Writing Process," (page 91). Make a transparency of the same diagram.

PRESENTING THE LESSON

1 After your class has studied the three states of matter, set up a table in front of the classroom that contains an example of each state. Explain that you are going to call students up to the table, one group at a time.

2 Each student will select one state of matter to observe. Then, each will call on his or her knowledge about that state of matter, the components of a well-crafted snapshot, and the phases of the writing process, in order to write a snapshot. Brainstorm criteria for the snapshot writing (for instance, vivid description and use of simile).

3 Give each student three minutes for self-coaching. Remind students that when a writer self-coaches, he or she can talk to him or herself, or jot down notes (not complete sentences), or sketch ideas on paper.

4 Provide each student with a copy of "Phases of the Writing Process" and/or place your transparency on the overhead for student reference. Explain that you will monitor the time allowed for each phase, but that writers are expected to work through each phase independently, checking off the tasks within a phase as they work.

Teacher's Notes: Snapshot knowledge gave the students a quick way to use all phases of the writing process. Once they are familiar with snapshot writing, students can apply this understanding to their content area knowledge during each phase of the writing process. Here are a few samples of the students' work.

All About Ice

Ice is cold! Ice is a solid and a solid keeps its shape. The reason ice is a solid is because of the atoms, they hardly move. They only vibrate like a slowly moving massage chair. They get close together like a football team planning a play. So if you put water into a freezer it will turn into a solid. If you touch ice it feels like putting your bare hands in the crispy, freezing snow. When ice is at room temperature it begins to melt. If you eat a popsicle it starts to melt like ice cycles dripping steadily on a warm winter's day.

Sydney

Winter Ice

The ice is slick like an ice rink,
And breaks like glass at a stone.
Listen! A snowflake lands on grass,
Then remains as water still cold from
the freeze.
I still remember that summer breeze.
If you listen closely you just might hear,
The crackling of ice with a summer's glare.
This is a snowflake.
Its molecules are frozen,
Yet, when it turns to liquid from solid,
Its atoms shoot up like rockets.
This is matter on a winter's day,
And now I go to play in the snow!
Hurray! Hurray!

Jonathon

Ice

This is a clear, cold solid. A solid has a definite shape and has matter. It is frozen water. When you put it up to your ear like a sea shell you hear crackling noises. It is a hard solid. If you keep the ice out too long in air hotter than 32° F. or 0° C., it will melt. It slips and slides in your hand like a fish out of water. The ice feels like the car door handle on an early winter morning. When you eat it, if it's thick it's crunchy like potato chips. Your mouth gets really, really cold and sometimes your face turns as red as an apple. It can also be very thin. You can crunch it up in your hand. The atoms and molecules stay together and move very slowly like kids at recess on a cold afternoon.

Rachel

Water Vapor

Water vapor is a gas. You have to heat it up to 212° Fahrenheit. When it is that temperature bubbles build up and jump out of the pot like rabbits being chased by a hunter. You can keep on heating it up until the pot is empty like a hunter going home without his dinner. Water vapor is made of H_2O like water and ice. Water vapor molecules move fast when they're heated up like a cheetah running after his dinner.

Jamie

Source of this lesson: Betsy Dulhanty, 4th grade teacher, Lebanon Community Schools, Perry-Worth Elementary School, Lebanon, Indiana

Science or Social Studies Lesson: Test Question Make-Over*

PURPOSE OF THE LESSON

To help students craft short-answer responses to test or quiz questions that include clear and detailed descriptions. (A quiz or test is a actually a published document; students should be expected to write well-crafted responses and apply their knowledge of each phase of the writing process to this assignment.)

PREPARING FOR THE LESSON

* ☀ Be prepared to administer a quiz or test with short answer responses.
* ☀ Make a copy of the "Phases of the Writing Process" diagram (page 91) for each student. Make a transparency of the same diagram.

PRESENTING THE LESSON

1 Explain to the class that today they will be taking a quiz (this could be in either science or social studies class). Remind students that when they are asked for a short essay type response, they are expected to write it with clear, detailed description as they do when writing a snapshot. Brainstorm criteria for test question content and rubric (clearly-stated content, several supporting details, use of a simile or metaphor).

2 Explain that for this test, when test-takers respond to the question, they can plan orally, web some ideas (not in complete sentences), or sketch an idea.

3 Give each student a copy of "Phases of the Writing Process" and/or place your transparency on the overhead for student reference. Explain that you will monitor the time allowed for each phase, but they are to work independently through each phase, checking off each task within a phase.

Teacher's Notes: When I started expecting more from their writing, students began to think more carefully about their responses. Before this lesson, many students had been responding with scanty information; they were using phrases instead of full-sentence responses. Now, responses are more detailed and more clearly expressed. I think the focus on figurative language helped my students understand the science (social studies) concepts in a more effective way.

When I required them to apply the phases of the writing process—first revision, second revision and editing—their responses began showing up grammatically correct. It all boils down to a teacher's expectations. Here are before-and-after samples of students' writing to the question, "Why is sunlight important to an ecosystem?"

Two Sixth-Graders' Before-and-After Test Responses

Before:

Sunlight is necessary for photosynthesis. Photosynthesis is necessary for ecosystem because this is how it gets its food for animals, plants, and soil. Without plants or algae providing food, there are not very many organisms that could survive.

After:

Sunlight is important to an ecosystem because it is necessary for photosynthesis to take place. Photosynthesis is the process in which plants use water, carbon dioxide, and sunlight to make food. Other living things eat the plants to obtain energy. If there was no sunlight, there wouldn't be plants for other living things to eat. Photosynthesis is like a baking recipe, and its ingredients are sunlight, water, and carbon dioxide.

Alex

Before:

Sunlight is necessary to an ecosystem because if there were no sunlight the plants would have no light to use for photosynthesis. So the herbivores would not survive because the plants would die. So the herbivores would not be able to eat so they would die. Then the carnivores would die because there would not be enough to feed all of them.

After:

Sunlight is necessary to an ecosystem because if there were no sunlight the plants would not have any light to use for photosynthesis. So the plants would die and the herbivores would not have any food source. They would die off, too. Then there would not be enough meat for the carnivores, so they would eat each other until they would die off, too. Also, they would not have enough oxygen because there is no photosynthesis. Oxygen is to fire as sunlight is to photosynthesis.

Marley

* *Source of this lesson*: Andy Seward, 6th-grade science and language arts teacher, Zionsville Community School Corporation, Zionsville Lower Middle School, Zionsville, Indiana

Language Arts Lesson: The Second Revision Challenge*

PURPOSE OF THE LESSON

To help students focus on second revision as they independently apply their knowledge about writing a well-crafted text and use all phases of the writing process.

PREPARING FOR THE LESSON

* ☀ Select 30 or 40 photographs cut from photography books or magazines.
* ☀ Make a copy for each student of the Lesson 11 Study Sheet, "Writing Coach's Prompt," page 58.
* ☀ Make a copy for each student of the diagram, "Phases of the Writing Process," page 91.

PRESENTING THE LESSON

1 Organize students in groups of 6 to 8 with their desks grouped together.

2 Place a stack of photographs face down in the center of the desks. Have each student select one photo that he or she wishes to write about. Ask students to use a folder to hide the selected photo so that other students do not see it.

3 Give each student a copy of the Lesson 11 Study Sheet, "Writing Coach's Prompt." After studying the photo carefully, students should use the study sheet to coach themselves through the planning of their snapshots.

4 Give each student a copy of "Phases of the Writing Process" and instruct them to use the sheet as a checklist. After each phase is completed they should check:

* ☀ drafting
* ☀ second revision
* ☀ formal publication
* ☀ first revision
* ☀ editing

5 Place all photos, face down, back into a stack on the table. Mix the photos up, then turn them face up on the table or the center of the desks.

6 Ask a student to read his or her snapshot aloud. Afterward, listeners from the group are to identify the photo described by the writer. If the listeners cannot identify the photo, the writer may need to engage in further second revision.

Teacher's Note: Using the "Photo to Snapshot" strategy allows my students to write a text that matches state rubric requirements. Students get excited and motivated to write when classmates can pick out the correct photo. Students keep asking me to let them use this strategy. It pleases me that my students actually ask to write. Here is an example of one student's snapshot.

One Student's Snapshot

    Little Cloud is a ten year old Native American. Her long black hair weaves around her shoulders as if it were trying to play with her. Her bangs shade her eyes. Sometimes she blows on her bangs so people will be able to see her sparkling blue eyes. Some say her eyes look like sapphires. Others say her eyes look like pebbles that had been hiding under the great river. Little Cloud's skin is soft and dark. Her cheeks are rosy and pink, and her mother named her Little Cloud because her cheeks looked like small clouds.

    Today, Little Cloud is wearing a white dress that has a lovely pattern on it. The pattern is gray, white, and black. Hugging around her waist is a silver shiny belt. It was her grandmother's when she was little. Little Cloud loves the belt. The design reminds her of her grandmother. Her body feels warm because of the pads on her legs. Her pads are deer skin, her favorite! She loves the feeling of the fur rubbing against her legs as she runs. While Little Cloud sits weaving, she looks at the bracelet that her grandmother had given her two summers ago. It is blue and it was shaped like a flower. The color was fading, but Little Cloud doesn't care. Finally, she calls to her mother, "I'm done weaving!"

DeAmber

Grade 5

* *Source of this lesson*: Kelly Wilson, 5th grade teacher, Lebanon Community Schools, Central Elementary School, Lebanon, Indiana

References

Further Reading for Teachers

You may wish to read more about the writing process and how fellow teachers developed writing workshop style classrooms. Listed below are some books recommended for further reading by teachers who are working to change how they teach writing. Also included are books that have influenced my thinking as I developed the ideas and content for this book.

Atwell, Nanci. (1998). *In the Middle: New Understandings About Writing, Reading, and Learning.* Second edition. Portsmouth, NH: Boynton/Cook.

Calkins, Lucy McCormick. (1994). *The Art of Teaching Writing.* Portsmouth, NH: Boynton/Cook.

Fletcher, Ralph. (1996). *Breathing In, Breathing Out—Keeping a Writer's Notebook.* Portsmouth, NH: Heinemann.

_____. (1999). *Live Writing, Breathing Life into Your Words.* New York, NY: Avon Books.

Fletcher, Ralph and JoAnn Portalupi. (1998). *Craft Lessons: Teaching Writing K–8.* York, ME: Stenhouse.

Frank, Marjorie. (1995). *If You're Trying to Teach Kids How to Write…You've Gotta Have This Book!* Second edition. Nashville, TN: Incentive Publications.

Goldberg, Natalie. (1986). *Writing Down the Bones: Freeing the Writer Within.* Boston: Shambhala Publications.

Graves, Donald H. (1994). *A Fresh Look at Writing.* Portsmouth, NH: Heinemann.

Portalupi, JoAnn and Ralph Fletcher. (2001). *Nonfiction Craft Lessons: Teaching Information Writing K–8.* York, ME: Stenhouse.

Robb, Laura. (1999). *Brighten Up Boring Beginnings and Other Quick Writing Lessons: 10–15 Minute Mini-Lessons and Reproducible Activities That Sharpen Students' Writing Skills.* New York, NY: Scholastic Professional Books.

_____. (1999). *Easy Mini-Lessons for Building Vocabulary: Practical Strategies that Boost Word Knowledge and Reading Comprehension.* New York, NY: Scholastic Professional Books.

_____. (1998). *Easy-to-Manage Reading and Writing Conferences: Practical Ideas for Making Conferences Work.* New York, NY; Scholastic Professional Books.

_____. (2000). *Teaching Reading in Middle School: A Strategic Approach to Teaching Reading That Improves Comprehension and Thinking.* New York, NY: Scholastic Professional Books.

Romano, Tom. (2000). *Blending Genre, Altering Style: Writing Multi-Genre Papers.* Portsmouth, NH: Heinemann.

Sabin, William A. (2001). *The Gregg Reference Manual.* Ninth edition. New York: Glencoe McGraw-Hill.

Short, Kathy G., Jerome C. Harste, and Carolyn Burke. (1996). Second edition. *Creating Classrooms for Authors and Inquirers.* Portsmouth, NH: Heinemann.

Spandel, Vicki. (2001). *Creating Writers: Through 6-Trait Writing Assessment and Instruction.* Third edition. New York: Addison Wesley Longman.

_____. (2001). *Books, Lessons, and Ideas for Teaching the Six Traits: Writing in the Elementary and Middle Grades.* Wilmington, MA: Great Source Education Group.

Sweeney, Jacqueline. (1995). *350 Fabulous Writing Prompts: Thought-Provoking Springboards for Creative, Expository, and Journal Writing*. New York, NY: Scholastic Professional Books.

Wells, Gordon. (1986). *The Meaning Makers, Children Learning Language and Using Language to Learn*. Portsmouth, NH: Heinemann.

Wilson, Jeni and Jan Lesley Wing. (1993). *Thinking for Themselves: Developing Strategies for Reflective Learning*. Portsmouth, NH: Heinemann.

On Editing

Clark, Roy Peter. (1995). *Free to Write—A Journalist Teaches Young Writers*. Portsmouth, NH: Heinemann.

Hall, Nigel and Anne Robinson. (1996). *Learning About Punctuation*. Portsmouth, NH: Heinemann.

Strunk, William, Jr. and E. B. White. (2000). *The Elements of Style*. Fourth edition. Boston: Allyn and Bacon.

On Second Revision

Lane, Barry. (1993). *After THE END*. Portsmouth, NH: Heinemann.

_____. (1996). *Lessons in Revision with Barry Lane, Volume One: The Power of Detail*, Grades 5–8 (video). Portsmouth, NH: Heinemann.

Classroom Collection for Students

Grammar textbooks and sets of classroom dictionaries are only a few of the resources that can benefit students. Ideally, students should be surrounded with a bounty of reference materials.

Many teachers obtain at least one copy of the various types of books listed below and place them into a supplemental reference collection kept in the classroom. Students use the books in the collection to locate needed information, read and discuss the information, and finally use the information to solve second revision and editing questions. Remember—students are inquirers and researchers during the writing process. They are applying their thinking and problem-solving skills to learn about grammar rules, spelling rules, how to expand their vocabularies, and other issues related to second revision and editing. The more resources available to them during these activities, the broader and deeper will be their success.

Your classroom resource collection should include:

- ☀ classroom set of dictionaries
- ☀ classroom set of grammar books
- ☀ atlases, maps, gazetteers
- ☀ phone book
- ☀ book of names
- ☀ various types and difficulty levels of dictionaries (regular and spelling)
- ☀ various types and difficulty levels of thesauruses
- ☀ your own collection of high school/college dictionaries, thesauruses, and grammar books

Here's a list of recommended dictionaries, thesauruses, and grammar books, as described in the *Scholastic Supplementary Materials Pre-K–8 Catalog*. Other helpful resources are listed at the end.

Dictionaries and Thesauruses (available from Scholastic Inc.)

Scholastic Science Dictionary, Grades 3–8. (Melvin Berger) New York, NY: Scholastic, Inc.
From abdomen to zygote, this kid-friendly, alphabetical and easy-to-use dictionary helps students with even the most difficult concepts while making their learning experience fascinating and fun! Over 2, 400 entries and 250 full-color illustrations

Scholastic Atlas of the United States, Grades 3 and Up
The essential, up-to-date geography resource for your classroom!

Scholastic Visual Dictionary, Grades 3 and Up
Whether a child needs to know the parts of a frog or the parts of a violin, this beautifully illustrated resource, with over 5,000 specialized vocabulary words and 700 illustrations in 350 subjects, is the perfect tool for helping children and language learners of all ages expand their vocabularies.

Scholastic Children's Dictionary, Grades 3–8
This dictionary contains more than 30,000 entries, sample sentences about real-life situations, complete Braille and American Sign Language Alphabets, pictures of most recent flags, and several maps.

Scholastic Children's Thesaurus (John K. Ballard)
Useful for expanding students' vocabulary, this innovative thesaurus does more than list synonyms and antonyms—it defines each headword and synonym and provides a sample sentence for each! Includes 500 head words and 2,500 synonyms and information boxes for students who want to know more.

Scholastic Dictionary of Spelling (Marvin Terban)
The only spelling dictionary just for kids, with alphabetically listed spellings, helpful spelling rules and tricks, humorous drawings, and a misspeller's dictionary.

The Scholastic Dictionary of Idioms (Marvin Terban)
With definitions and origins for over 600 everyday American sayings and expressions, this appealing reference book includes sample sentences, a substantive cross-referencing index, and amusing illustrations.

The Scholastic Rhyming Dictionary (Sue Young)
This kid-friendly source of rhymes for poetry, prose, and songwriting is organized by vowel sounds and final syllables. Students will enjoy writing their own rhymes and poetry.

Scholastic Treasury of Quotations for Children (Adrienne Betz)
With over 1,200 memorable quotations, this unique resource covers seven engaging categories such as courage, honesty, and friendship. Supplemental information includes details on phrase origins, a bibliographical index of 700 famous speakers, and hints on how students can use quotations effectively in their own writing.

Grammar Books (available from Scholastic Inc.)

Punctuation Power (Marvin Terban)
One of the only punctuation guides available to children ages 8–14, this new addition to the Scholastic Guides series uses clever, learner-friendly example sentences designed to make learning punctuation fun.

Checking Your Grammar (Marvin Terban)
> Written in a light, appealing style, this guide is packed with information on parts of speech, spelling rules, punctuation, and much more.

Comic-Strip Grammar, Grades 4–8 (Dan Greenberg)
> Reproducible cartoons introduce and explain a simple grammar rule or concept and then challenge students to apply the concept with engaging practice exercises.

25 Great Grammar Poems with Activities, Grades 3–6 (Bobbi Katz)
> Reproducible poems that focus on a key topic—parts of speech, capitalization, punctuation, sentence structure.

Writing With Style (Sue Young)
> This writing guide shows students how to plan, produce, polish, and present more sophisticated written work, for better grades and more personal satisfaction.

Putting It in Writing (Steve Otfinoski)
> This refreshing and accessible guide uses student writing samples to show how to compose different types of letters and reports.

Books on Parts of Speech

These books by Ruth Heller can be used as read-aloud experiences or for students to read and discuss as they meet in small grammar-study groups.

Heller, Ruth. (1998). *A Cache of Jewels, and Other Collective Nouns.* New York, NY: Grosset & Dunlap.

_____. (1998). *Kites Sail High—A Book About Verbs.* New York, NY: Grosset & Dunlap.

_____. (1998). *Many Luscious Lillipops—A Book About Adjectives.* New York, NY: Grosset & Dunlap.

_____. (1998). *Merry-Go-Round—A Book About Nouns.* New York, NY: Grosset & Dunlap.

_____. (1998). *Up, Up and Away—A Book About Adverbs.* New York, NY: Grosset & Dunlap.

Books of Names

Altman, Nathaniel. (1999). *The Little Giant Encyclopedia of Names.* Sterling Publication.

Lasky, Bruce. (1995). *The Very Best Baby Name Book in the Whole World.* New York, NY: Simon and Schuster.

Shaw, Lisa. (1997). *The Everything Baby Names Book.* Holbrook, MA: Adams Media Corporation.

Atlases

Dorling Kindersley Limited. (2000). *Dorling Kindersley Children's Atlas.* New York, NY: Dorling Kindersely.
> *Well-illustrated introduction to atlases for children.*

MacMilllan/McGraw-Hill. (1997). *World Atlas for Intermediate Students.* New York, NY: MacMillan/McGraw-Hill.
> *Describes, through maps, tables, graphs, and text, the ways people live with each other and the earth.*

National Geographic Society. (1996). *National Geographic World Atlas for Young Explorers.* Washington, D.C.: National Geographic Society.
> *Presents world, regional, and thematic maps as well as photographic essays on each continent.*

Steele, Phillip. (1997). *The Kingfisher Young People's Atlas of the World.* New York, NY: Kingfisher.
> *Introduces the places and people of the world through maps, facts, and photographs.*